India

An Anthology of Contemporary Writing

Edited by
DAVID RAY and AMRITJIT SINGH

Photographs by
MADAN MAHATTA

A *New Letters* Book
University of Missouri - Kansas City

SWALLOW PRESS
OHIO UNIVERSITY PRESS
Chicago   Athens, Ohio   London

Publication of this edition is supported by a grant from the National Endowment for the Arts, a federal agency. The Indo-American Fellowship Program, sponsored by the Governments of India and the U.S., was most helpful in bringing the editors together. The editors would also like to express thanks to those who helped gather the material for this anthology: Keki Daruwalla, Paul Engle, Nissim Ezekiel, Francine E. Krishna, Jayanta Mahapatra, Keshav Malik, and Meenakshi Mukherjee. Valuable assistance in editorial reading, proofreading, etc., was given by Faye Callahan, Marilyn Cannaday, Elaine Goodwin, Lois Harvey, Ved Prakash, R. D. Sharma, Ram Krishna Sharma, Sadashiv Shrotriya, and R. Surianarayanan. Judy Ray shared editorial labors and prepared the design and lay-out for this book, while Robert Stewart co-ordinated work done on two continents. The co-operation of the American Center, the Sahitya Akademi, and Fulbright House in New Delhi is also gratefully acknowledged. Publication of this book has also depended upon the support and co-operation of the University of Missouri—Kansas City and the University of Rajasthan, Jaipur.

ISBN 8214-0736-8

Ohio University Press/Swallow Press
Scott Quad, Dept. FRDR
Athens, OH 45701

Authors and Translators:

To The Reader

Our selection of writing from and about India has been put together primarily for the reader outside India, but we hope it will also have appeal and relevance within India. We have gathered together a sampler both in English and from the other languages such as Bengali, Dogri, Hindi, Kannada, Kashmiri, Konkani, Malayalam, Marathi, Oriya, Punjabi, Tamil and Urdu. It would be fallacious, by the way, to regard any one of these languages (including English and Hindi) as having special priority or superiority: all the regional literatures are vital and treasured modes of expression, and it has been noted by critics that those writers who have kept to their regional languages often express themselves with power denied all but the most exceptional writers in English. For some reason, possibly the spectre of censorship, these writers more frequently address the problems of politics and protest; and of course each language stresses its own idiom, the customs of its region, the rich fund of its geography and myth.

Bilingualism or multilingualism is not a new Indian phenomenon. For an American to eavesdrop on a phone conversation in India, when the speaker begins in English, weaves in and out of Hindi, then switches to Punjabi when he discovers that the other speaker is from the Punjab, is an experience that emphasizes both the cultural power of multilingualism and its potential for fragmenting or integrating experience. Both the positive and negative sides of this ability are present as forces in today's India. At its worst, the tentativeness of Hindi as a national language has created a tower of Babel. At its best, respect for regionalism and variety keeps traditions alive that should not die, and slows the inevitable erosion of language groups.

Our main purpose, when we began gathering work for this collection was to bring together in one volume the best and most readable of the poems and short stories available to us as editors. We were sitting in Jaipur, India, in February, 1982, appreciative of the halcyon weather—much like Arizona's winter—and aware that America was having some of its worst blizzards in years. We decided to exorcize our guilt at such good fortune (we could swim outdoors or stroll about under blossoming trees) by assuming the purely voluntary chore of reading thousands of manuscripts in order to find the few we wanted to share with our readers in America. As one discovery led to another, we expanded our search to permit the inclusion of impressive writings that had appeared in Indian journals like *Vagartha* and *Chandrabhaga. New Letters* prints only original work, but we felt that we should not deny, on a technicality, an appearance to a story or poem that would otherwise be lost to an American audience. We wanted our criteria to be unrestrictive, wanted to choose a piece only on the basis of its excellence. If it had not been printed in the United States, we considered it eligible; still, most of the work here has been set from manuscript.

If we shared an editorial bias, it was toward giving priority to work that deals concretely and authentically with the Indian social reality. For the two of us, this bias merely reflects convictions voiced in our own writing: a literary work is not merely a verbal construct, an exercise in cleverness. It should confront issues larger than its creator, should reflect more than his subjectivity, and should survive independently of his personality. These works have, consequently, much more chance of being read on their own merits—by those who know little about the authors. All too often in America the cult around the writer takes precedence over the value of the work. We looked for and found manuscripts that embody deeply felt perceptions of changing social reality. And yet, both in India and the United States, those who choose to write of real life problems with boundaries larger than narcissism are likely to be banished from the print culture and neglected by the leading critics who opt for safe expressions of *animus* and *anima.*

Censorship is a real problem in both countries—the two largest democracies in the world—although its contours and modes of operation may differ drastically. As Alexander Solzhenitsyn noted in his Harvard address a few years ago, the standard method of censorship in America (though there are occasional book-burnings in Wisconsin and elsewhere) is simply to deny a writer access to the media, to impose involuntary silence or to limit his audience through non-support. The melodox (orthodox, mellow) triumphs while individualism is honed into the agreeable. As Herbert Marcuse has noted, it is quite possible to kill the power of art with kindness. In the United States, where opportunities for patronage at a price abound, the problem is a real one. In India, censorship is not always so subtle, and recent instances have been brutally dramatic—e.g., one politician recently began beating a poet on the head with a shoe. The poet no doubt learned more clearly, perhaps, than his American counterpart how to distinguish friend from foe. The foe shall forever after be designated as the listener who gets up and begins pounding the poet on the head, or the reader who in his heart would like to do so.

As two who have lived in India (one for most of a lifetime, the other for most of a year), have experienced its splendors and squalors, and share hope for its immense potential, we wanted to offer a book that reflects our feeling for this fabulously beautiful country, as well as for its mind-boggling problems, apparent to any observer and documented regularly and powerfully by *India Today* and *The Illustrated Weekly of India*, weekly magazines that are unfortunately seldom available in the United States. The country is confounding to American visitors, heirs of pragmatism and proponents of the belief that most problems can be solved. It is inconceivable for an American to accept the idea that many age-old evils, built into the social structure, will go forever unchanged, and that clearly improvable conditions will go on getting worse. An American, watching the morning excremental pollution of the Ganges concurrent with its ritual bathing, might suggest a halt to such a practice; an Indian would know that such a crusade would be doomed—a man might as well fight the tides or try doing something about the country's population explosion (doubled in the last twenty-five years and due to double again by 2000 A.D., assuring that some sixty cities will be as big and unliveable as Bombay and Calcutta are).

Jack Armstrong and The Rover Boys would concur with John Stuart Mill, Ben Franklin, and John Dewey in putting a stop to police brutality (broken legs, eyes put out), village dacoities (massacres of Harijan caste untouchables), such rituals as bride-burning (of those who have not brought enough dowry), the kidnapping of children for beggary, or the buying and selling of women for prostitution. There has always been, in the Westerner's perception of the East, a certain amount of horrific awe: one thinks of the early accounts of travellers who witnessed *suttee* or, in the times of Queen Elizabeth, the splendors and cruelties of Akbar's court at Fatehpur Sikri, whose pink stone ruins are still a must for every tourist.

For better or for worse, the writer in India has few of the opportunities that abound in the United States, little or no income from readings and publications, no creative writing courses, and no retreats or fellowships for pursuit of his own work. Even a major prize like the annual Sahitya Akademi award, rich in prestige, is very small in comparison with prizes in England, America, Australia, Canada, and New Zealand. Nor do English departments help much. Quite the contrary, they compound neglect with their snobberies, their worship of Eliot, Stevens and Frost, a perspective that until recently excluded even the livelier American literature and that of the Third World. They can be blamed too for their indifference to students and their hostility to originality, for their insistence on teaching work more relevant to themselves than to their students, and for their vested interest in obscurity. On the other hand, students, whose frenetic unrest is an index of a larger national confusion of purpose, make it easier to dismiss their seriousness: the campus in India is generally anarchic, with students acting like a swarm of bees, keeping themselves in perpetual turmoil, not in protest over serious issues that will determine the country's future, but over exam schedules or hostel privileges. And yet one gets every now and then a strong sense of their unchannelled energy, their potential dynamism. If redirected, that energy could save their society, if not the world. Thus, this anthology is dedicated to the youth of India.

DAVID RAY & AMRITJIT SINGH
Jaipur, June 1982

Five Poems

NISSIM EZEKIEL

Guru

The saint, we are told,
once lived a life of sin—
nothing spectacular, of course,
just the usual things.
We smile, we are not surprised.
Unlikely though it seems,
we too one day
may grow up like him,
dropping our follies
like old clothes or creeds.

But then we learn
the saint is still a faithless friend,
obstinate in argument,
ungrateful for favors done,
hard with servants and the poor,
discourteous to disciples, especially men,
condescending, even rude
to visitors (except the foreigners)
and overscrupulous in checking
the accounts of the ashram.
He is also rather fat.

Witnessing the spectacle
we no longer smile.
If saints are like this
what hope is there then for us?

In The Garden

It seemed to me so much like you,
To find the planning of the garden
Faulty, and the birds too few.

Your walk was slow, informal there
Among the trees whose names you knew,
And flowers commonplace or rare.

The elephant of broken stone
Deserved, you said, a closer view
Than animals of flesh and bone.

The spacious lawns with sand defined
Where children shouted, breezes blew,
Or water like a lucid mind

Negotiates obstructive rocks;
And bridges modestly designed;
Were better than the tower of clocks,

And hedges ruining every view—
At which I felt your kindness harden:
It seemed to me so much like you.

In the Country Cottage

That night the lizard came
our indolence was great;
we went to bed before
our eyes were heavy, limbs
prepared to stretch or love.

Immobile, tense and grey,
he taught us patience as
he waited for the dark.
From time to time we could
not help but glance at him

and learn again that he
was more alive than us
in silent energy,
though his aim was only
the death of cockroaches.

When we awoke the next
morning we found as we
expected that the job
was done, clean and complete,
and the stout lizard gone.

A Morning Walk

Driven from his bed by troubled sleep
In which he dreamt of being lost
Upon a hill too high for him
(A modest hill whose sides grew steep),
He stood where several highways crossed
And saw the city, cold and dim,
Where only human hands sell cheap.

It was an old, recurring dream,
That made him pause upon a height.
Alone, he waited for the sun,
And felt his blood a sluggish stream.
Why had it given him no light,
His native place he could not shun,
The marsh where things are what they seem?

Barbaric city sick with slums,
Deprived of seasons, blessed with rains,
Its hawkers, beggars, iron-lunged,
Processions led by frantic drums,
A million purgatorial lanes,
And child-like masses, many-tongued,
Whose wages are in words and crumbs.

He turned away. The morning breeze
Released no secrets to his ears.

The more he stared the less he saw
Among the individual trees.
The middle of his journey nears.
Is he among the men of straw
Who think they go which way they please?

Returning to his dreams, he knew
That everything would be the same.
Constricting as his formal dress,
The pain of his fragmented view.
Too late and small his insights came,
And now his memories oppress,
His will is like the morning dew.

The garden on the hill is cool,
Its hedges cut to look like birds
Or mythic beasts are still asleep.
His past is like a muddy pool
From which he cannot hope for words.
The city wakes, where fame is cheap,
And he belongs, an active fool.

For Elkana

The warm April evening
tempts us to the breezes
sauntering across the lawn.
We drag our chairs down
the stone steps and plant them there
unevenly, to sit or rather sprawl
in silence till the words begin to come.
My wife, as is her way,
surveys the scene, comments
on a broken window-pane,
suggests a thing or two
that every husband in the neighborhood
knows exactly how to do
except of course the man she loves,
who happens to be me.

Unwilling to dispute
the obvious fact
that she is always right,
I turn towards the more
attractive view that opens up
behind my eyes and shuts her out.
Her voice crawls up and down the lawn,
our son, who is seven,
hears it — and it reminds him of something.
He stands before us,
his small legs apart,
crescent-moon-like chin uplifted
eyes hard and cold
to speak his truth
in masterly determination:
Mummy, I want my dinner, now.
Wife and husband in unusual rapport
share one unspoken thought:
Children Must Be Disciplined.
She looks at me. I look away.
The son is waiting. In another second
he will repeat himself.
Wife wags a finger,
firmly delivers a verdict: Wait.
In five minutes I'll serve you dinner.
No, says the little one,
not in five minutes, now.
I am hungry.
It occurs to me the boy is like his father.
I love him as I love myself.
Wait, darling, wait,
Mummy says wait for five minutes.
I won't be hungry any more.
This argument appeals to me.
Such a logician deserves his dinner
        straightaway.
My wife's delightful laughter
holds the three of us together.
We rise and go into the house.

Homecoming

DHRUVAKUMAR JOSHI

I had to leave the shores
that they should see fit
to do me honor.
Now, accounts of my passage
through the Golden Gate
adorn drawing-room gossip-shelves.

Advice they want on how
to squeeze a passage
to a University on an assistantship.

Sneakily, in the other room,
daughters (ripe and waiting)
are chaperoned before me.

Friends who mocked
at my exercise of freedom once
now pat me.

Fathers and mothers
uncles and aunts
cousins-in-law

scan me like customs men, before
certifying me fit
for their homely girl.

A brief exile is all I had.
It is over. And that
has made all the difference.

Three Poems

KEKI N. DARUWALLA

The Middle Ages

Returning as the leaves fell off the year's branches
returning as the light swung low into the eyes
to the blindings in Bhagalpur,
the pot-hole in the middle of the eyes;
someone astraddle on another's chest,
left thumb working the eye into a bulge,
the right hand holding a cycle spoke,
I asked how long can fancy indulge
in such macabre stills? Then news of killers
at the door as cries rang loud
and the males fled. Mother and children cowered.
The hamlet ran short of shrouds.
Helicopters descended before the vultures could.
Journals were full of obituaries.
One hour of being truly brutalized
is worth a lifetime of anonymous misery.
How was it that listening to accounts
of Harijans slaughtered in the villages
my hands started rummaging among dusty shelves
for some dark volume on the Middle Ages?

Not walls emblazoned with heraldic signs
caught my eye, nor crusaders crossing the waters
but a wretch condemned, bought by the town of Mons
for the public pleasure of seeing him quartered.
Tithe and levy driving the people mad
as the tourniquet tightened. Memory thrives
on a scene, Parisian heralds
announcing an impost and fleeing for their lives.
And plague, the vengeance of the Lord, that pressed
upon the spirit, as these domed reactors
squat on ours. In their frenzies they never knew
if it was God's curse, rat-flea or vector
that brought it on. Smoke-pots burned in the house
and for remedies, powdered staghorn was enjoined,

and crushed pearl, myrrh and saffron. And still
next day buboes covered the armpit and the groin.
Doctors were important, they went about
in purple gowns and belts of silver thread,
the medieval versions of our saviour,
those who will avert war and lower the price of bread.

And so I take heart from the Middle Ages
as time runs out on us;
as some future being rained off under an acid-drizzle
will derive solace from us.

Migrations

You don't have people now
who can sense a drought
from the way frost crinkles
on the ground in February,
a leaf leans into the wind,
or the miasmal drift
of plumed grass or burst bulrushes.
Hence this surprise today
at the tracery of earth-cracks
seen through blackened stubble.

It was sixty years back, and I a child,
terrified, as he stood at our door,
tribal-dark and thick-lipped.
God had riveted his bones well,
for they didn't fall apart,
ankle, knee and hip-joint
angling out of his parchment skin.
He was silhouette-still and silhouette-black;
even his eyes didn't move as I ran in.
Mother, churning her butter-milk
asked me to give him a tumbler.
Gingerly I held out a clay urn
lest our fingers touch.
He drank and left, soundless,
a vision creeping away
from a hardening eyeball.

Later there were thousands;
footsore hordes scouring the land for forage,
men enough to start a tiger-beat
in every nullah. And herds,
first camels and then goats
which hugged the stems with forepaws
and nibbled away, till the trees
were left only with a green head of hair.

Well, the wheel's come full circle, as they say.
Do you see trains steaming out
ten thousand frying on the lurching roofs?
It is our carts rolling today
our villages walking out with their headloads,
an ant-line following
the scent of a moist root.

The Unrest Of Desire

The unrest of desire is lit up with eyes,
whatever the mask you slap upon your face,
however you tear at the soft throat of life
and probe the salt-blood with your insistent tongue.
The unrest of desire is revealed by eyes.

However you bury the shadow in the heart,
under slabs of concrete and a coil of bone,
however you wall the cave-impulse at the mouth,
it will hammer at the sides and break free—
however you bury the shadow in the heart.

You may etch the shadow on the cavern-wall
and turn the drives into aboriginie art,
bison and stag loping in charcoal lines.
You can't erase the burn. It will char your dreams,
however you bury the shadow in the heart.

Nine Poems On Arrival

ADIL JUSSAWALLA

Spiders infest the sky.
They are palms, you say,
hung in a web of light.

Gingerly, thinking of concealed
springs and traps, I step off the plane,
expect take-off on landing.

Garlands beheading the body
and everyone dressed in white.
Who are we ghosts of?

You. You. You.
Shaking hands. And you.

Cold hands. Cold feet. I thought
the sun would be lower here
to wash my neck in.

Contact. We talk a language of beads
along well-established wires.
The beads slide, they open, they
devour each other.

Some were important.
Is that one,
as deep and dead as the horizon?

Upset like water
I dive for my favorite tree
which is no longer there
though they've let its roots remain.

Dry clods of earth
tighten their tiny faces
in an effort to cry. Back
where I was born,
I may yet observe my own birth.

I Am A Poet

To know oneself truly is not an easy thing. If God had not granted me this long life, to reach my three score years and ten, this knowledge might have escaped me. I have, it is true, engaged myself in a series of activities. But the inmost me is not to be found in any of these. At the end of the journey I am able to see, a little more clearly, the orb of my life. Looking back the only thing of which I feel certain is that I am a poet.

I do not claim to be a theologian, a leader of men, a moral or a religious preceptor. I had once written: I have no desire to be a leader of the New Bengal. I meant it. The messengers of Truth's white Radiance, who purify earth, air and water, who guide men to the paths of peace, I honor them — and I know that my seat is not by their side. But when that one Radiance throws itself out into the many, scatters its splendor through the spectrum of this universal manifestation, then and there I find my vocation — as a poet. I am a voice of the expressive many, an endless, nameless delight that fathers-forth all things.

To cherish this delight, in the heart of creation, to express it in all ways of one's being, that indeed has been my labor. I do not presume to lead men to their life's goal. To travel alongside is happiness enough for me. Some have described me as a metaphysician, others have thrust upon me the doubtful role of a schoolmaster. But, led by my love of play, I have been indeed a truant. Not for me the teacher's job. I still remember the little boy in the early hours, the light struggling to break through dawn's veil of obscurity, setting out on life's long journey. The wonder has never ceased. The heart's lotus pool had stirred and shivered with the unknown mystery. It has left me, a wanderer, forever restless.

And now that I have turned seventy friends complain about my lightheartedness, it hurts their sense of propriety. But I can hardly afford to waste my time trying to do what is not in my nature to do. Through all the experience of these seventy years I have come to the conclusion that I was meant to be a companion of the Ever-changing. I do not know if I have achieved anything or if I shall leave anything worthwhile behind me. I crave not for permanence; he plays, but without attachment, the playhouse which he himself builds is also the one which he allows to fall by the wayside. The wings of storm have swept away yester evening's *alpona* designs in our mango grove, and they have to be laid afresh. If I have been able to supply a few toys to the world's playhouse I shall not care for their preservation in perpetuity. The potsherd will one day find its place on the scrapheap. Enough if I have been able to breathe life into these toys of time and charge them with the Bliss at the root of all that is. I ask for nothing more.

The expressive side of the Santiniketan *ashrama*, that alone is mine. It has no doubt its executive side, there are experts to look after that. What I had wished for was to give vent to the hunger for form, for human self-expression. And so I had looked for a forest retreat, or *tapovana*, as its proper ambiance. Not in the midst of sordid city-built houses, but under the blue canopy, from morn to eve, I had wished to be a playmate of these boys and girls. To express, growing out of this our common life, beauty's happy and blessed form that was my one and only concern. I have naturally had to introduce other utilitarian activities as well but you will not find me in these. I am where life is trying to express itself. The classes that I have started or taught here are secondary — my real work has been to help awaken, in nature's vast playground, the tender grace of childhood, its budding effort, the first rays of knowledge falling across its horizon. Otherwise I would have been swamped by the trivia of routine, statute and syllabus. My happiness, my only fulfilment has been in trying to rouse the young ones to the delight of the unseen Player, to set them in tune with the dance of life itself. It is not in me to be more serious than that. The Master of Games has mercifully released me from the fetters of the mature and the elder. Those who try to set me on a pedestal I tell them that I was born with my seat below, on the lap of the earth. In these trees and forests, the dust, earth and grass, have I poured out my whole life. Those who are close to the spirit of the earth, those who are made and shaped by her, and who will find their final rest in her, of them all I am the friend. I am a poet, *ami kavi*.

Translated from the Bengali by Sisirkumar Ghose

1996

RABINDRANATH TAGORE

Tell me, who are you,
idly reading this poem?
Can I send you, over those years,
just a touch of this morning in Spring?
Can you find the same jasmine renewed?
Can you sight the emerald green
of eight parrots in flight,
exactly one hundred years
from this moment, their path in the air
precisely the same, flung
like a necklace? I greet you,
words just slightly delayed,
held on the air
like a song passed on
by one singer, who teaches another.
Do what I ask you,
give me that sign of your friendship.
Go to the window, the South one,

stand on the balcony, touch the iron rail,
gaze out at the horizon, its clean line,
the shimmering seam of heaven and earth.
Then think of my love for you,
sailing and floating and finding you
by way of this poem, alive now
exactly one hundred years.
And think how far you have come
on that same road I walked.
Look back at the young:
they're behind you forever,
or before you, as you're before me.
And think how I burst into song,
just for you, how I touched
the red blossom, how my thoughts
unfolded one after another,
one hundred years back. And tell me,
does a poet sing to you now?
Can you give him your friendship?
I greet him, poet
still working, deep in his efforts
to make sense of the moon and the earth,
untangling lies from the cities.
He hears my song echo, knows
we are one, and these one hundred years
just a bridge. It's reached
over the years, links the knoll
where I pause, and the one where you stand.
It's strong. It's survived, anchored
in love. And has brought
this song forward, over
catastrophes, floods, immense
human losses. Breathe deep now,
pronounce my first name like a mantra,
draw in my spirit mingled with jasmine.
Don't wait any longer to sing.

Adapted by David Ray

The Questions of the Yaksha

The climax of the third book of *The Mahabharata* is where the God Dharma, in the guise of a crane, tests Yudhishthira, one of the Pandava brothers. The following is a selection of the questions and answers exchanged between the Spirit and Yudhishthira:

"What is greater than earth? What is higher than the heaven?"

"Mother is greater than earth; father is higher than the heaven."

"In what one thing is all *dharma* summed up? What single thing constitutes all fame? What sole means takes one to heaven?"

"Skill in the discharge of one's duties sums up all *dharma*; giving sums up all fame; truthfulness is the sole road to heaven; and good conduct is the one means to happiness."

"What is the foremost wealth?"

"Learning."

"What is the best gain?"

"Health."

"What is the supreme happiness?"

"Contentment."

"What is superior to all other *dharmas* in the world?"

"Benevolence."

"Whose control leads to absence of sorrow?"

"The control of mind!"

"Which friendship ages not?"

"That with good souls."

"By casting away what, does man become dear to others?"

"Pride."

"By abandoning what thing does man become rich?"

"Desire."

"By giving up what, does one become happy?"

"Avarice."

"What is penance?"

"Penance is the observance of one's own ordained duty."

"What is self-control?"
"Control of the mind."
"What is forbearance?"
"Putting up with opposites."
"What is shame?"
"Aversion to do a reprehensible act is shame."
"What is straightforwardness?"
"Equanimity."
"Who is the enemy hard to be won?"
"Anger."
"What is the endless disease?"
"Avarice."
"Who is said to be a good man?"
"He who is benevolent to all beings."
"Who is a bad man?"
"He who is barren of sympathy."
"What is gift?"
"Protection of life."
"What is the wonder of the world?"
"Everyday, live beings enter the abode of death;
those who remain think that they will survive; what
greater wonder is there than this?"
"What is the news in the world?"
"With earth as the pot, the firmament as the covering lid,
the sun as the fire, day and night as faggots
and the seasons and months as the stirring ladle,
Time cooks all beings; this is the great news."

Dear Madhuban

SHIRSENDU MUKHOPADHYAY

My head feels rather light these days—vacant, like an empty room. Only one or two sparrows come and go. This is quite all right. I am sure it is all right to be like this.

Only yesterday I got another anonymous letter. It says: "The rebel's path tends to turn back towards domesticity. From the forest, the ascetic returns home." It's written in red ink. There's no name or signature at the end, but I know the handwriting. It belongs to my friend Kunal Mitra who left home long ago and nobody knows his whereabouts. I've had no news of him for ten years.

The postmarks made by our inefficient postal department are never distinct. Yesterday I tried deciphering them with a magnifying glass all day and didn't succeed in making out from where the letter had been posted. But I know that whatever place he wrote this letter from, Kunal is not there any more. He will have moved again. Kunal roams from place to place like a wandering ascetic, and I wish I could know where he is right now.

Towards evening yesterday, when the sunlight had faded, I put down the magnifying glass. I had developed a headache by poring through the lens all day. I covered my tired eyes with my hands and sat still for a long time. No, that's wrong. I wasn't just covering my eyes. There were tears trickling down between my fingers.

The path of the rebel turns back towards domesticity. From the forest the ascetic returns home. These are my own words.

Kunal has merely returned them to me. I could almost see his mercilessly smiling face behind the words, almost hear him say: "You had shown me the way. You brought me out of the four walls. And now where have you gone back to, Madhuban? Whose left-over food are you licking now? Don't you feel ashamed?"

Kunal shoots these unerring arrow-words at me. It's like someone fighting from behind the clouds. He seems to change his place every day while I, Madhuban—I am tied down to a fixed address. Kunal has become a shadow or an illusion. I shall never trace him now. So there is no obligation to reply to his letters.

Last evening I didn't switch on the lights. I sat alone with Kunal's letter in my hand. There is a nest of lizards in my heart. Each time I think of leaving home, the lizards make ticking sounds and say: don't go. I know of course I'd never go. Yet my fingers are wet with tears. It wasn't for me but for Kunal that I cried. And then my head felt empty like a vacant room. Occasionally, like one or two sparrows, memories flitted in and out.

For quite some time I wasn't aware of what was happening around me. Then my wife Sona called out: "Raja, come here a second." I went in to find she was changing her clothes. She said, "Look. I haven't bothered you the whole day. But now you must tell me whose letter you've been brooding over so long?" I brought the letter and showed it to her. Glancing at it she casually threw it on the table. She said, "This awful blouse buttons down the back. I can't reach them. Raja, please do up the buttons for me." Then I noticed what Sona was wearing. The sleeves came up to the elbow and were edged with lace. I had seen her wear this blouse before, but she had never asked me to button it for her. I smiled and helped her with the buttons.

Very softly she said, "Oh, what cold hands!" "Cold?" I was surprised. "Why, no!" I touched her cheeks with my hands. She shook her head. "No, not that kind of cold. So indifferent." I stood there without speaking. Sona draped the sari round her body, then suddenly brought her face close to me and whispered, "Love?"

At that moment I forgot all about Kunal's letter. Sometime later I had to button her blouse again.

After that Sona picked up the letter from the table and said, "This letter in red ink—a letter of only a line and a half—what shall we do with it? Shall we frame it?"

"The joke's on me, Sona," I smiled. "I used to say these words once upon a time. After many years they've found their way back to me."

She was frowning at the letter. "Is this meant to frighten you?"

"Oh no," I shook my head and laughed. "It's just a game."

She hesitated a little and then said, "There is no name or address on the letter, but you seem to know who wrote it."

"Perhaps it's another self of mine, sending messages to me from the past."

"How poetic!" Sona smiled. "You are making poetry, Raja." Then, lowering her voice she spoke very slowly, "You used to tell me I am your other self. How many such selves do you have, Raja?"

Jealous. This home is Sona's kingdom. I am her king and she calls me Raja. I could never make her understand that at one time Kunal used to call me 'Dear Madhuban.'

No, I've no intention of going back in time in order to become 'Dear Madhuban' to Kunal again. I am quite all right as I am now, my head spacious and empty like a quiet room. Occasionally a few sparrows come and go. One or two memories. What more do I need? I like light and air, I like holidays, I like leisure. I love the sound of a sewing machine, the crying of my infant son, the dolls inside the glasscase, or flowers arranged in a vase; and the sound of the lizards in my heart which say: 'don't go.'

Yet, sometimes when I walk down crowded streets, I suddenly feel lost. Or if I wake up at midnight I find that my regrets have turned to stone. Occasionally, when I look into the mirror I am startled. Like drops of rain from some unreal space a few words drop into my mind. Alas, Madhuban, no one will ever know that you had come on this earth and lived.

All this, of course, is just sentiment. Actually I feel no very

clear regret. I don't really want to go back. Nor do I enjoy remi-
niscing. Only sometimes, when Sona goes out with the baby,
or stays overnight at her parents' house, I switch off the lights
in the evening and sit facing myself. Like mosquitoes buzzing
in the dark, a few thoughts murmur around me. I quickly try
to recall the sound of my son's cry, or listen in the silence for
an echo of Sona's voice. Slowly I recover. If once in a while
it seems to me that my life need not have been so placid, so
static, that I could have had a different, a distant, an uncertain
life, then I grab whatever object that is near me, a medicine
bottle, a pen, or if nothing is available I look at the stone on my
ring and try to focus my mind. I struggle to obliterate the past
and the future. I whisper to myself, "This is better. It's much
better to be like this." Then my head feels empty and very light
as if it is an open, vacant room.

The first of these anonymous letters in red ink arrived at my
address many years ago, soon after I had lost touch with Kunal.
It said: "In life it's not enough to be honest. Ideals are more
important. Unless you have ideals, you cannot be completely
honest." Each sentence ended with an exclamation mark. In fact
these statements were all concealed quotations. The exclamation
marks hit me like the points of so many needles. These words
were mine too, and they were being returned to me. That was
the first letter. Then, soon after my marriage, there was another:
"The protest march will have to disperse if it starts raining. To
save our skins we will have to run for shelter under the trees."
I do not know if by 'the trees' he meant the four banana trees in
the traditional ritual of marriage. I did not show this letter to
Sona. But since then I have known that Kunal knows all about
me, he keeps track of me and knows my address. He hasn't forgotten me. I was possessed by a mild fear. There were lots of
other things I'd taught him. Suppose he remembered them all?
Then, gradually, I realized I was wrong. Kunal was merely playing a game with me. He had discarded me from his life like an
old toy. Only, once in a while, he wanted to touch me from a
distance merely to see if he could startle me.

I must say Kunal had learnt the game rather well. All yesterday I felt like a different person. This morning, when Sona

opened her eyes, the first thing she did was to look at me and
ask, "Are you still thinking of that dreadful letter?" I was surprised, even though I wasn't really thinking of that letter, nor
of Kunal. "Are you crazy?" I answered with a smile. For some
time she moved about quietly in the room, tidying the bed,
folding the baby's nappies and putting up the mosquito net.
Then she came to me. "How long have you been sitting like
this at the window? I have never seen you get up so early."

That's true. I am not an early riser. I don't know what made
me wake up so early today. I couldn't go back to sleep. It was
cold outside, yet I left the warmth of the bed and sat at the
window. There was a thick mist outside; the road below seemed
like a quietly flowing river in the dim light. Distant Calcutta
seemed frozen in dew like a tall forest. As soon as I lit a cigarette a few old memories strayed in. I tried to resist them but
didn't succeed. Once, at dawn, a long time ago, I'd seen a hermit
in an ashram, his eyes closed, his right arm raised, utter his
morning prayer: "Beyond the darkness stands the great being of
indestructible color, manifest in auspicious symbols. Let us
bend at his feet, let us pray to him. Let us move in his direction."
It was not a hymn, merely words spoken slowly and distinctly.
That was many years ago. Even now I shiver when I remember
it: "Let us move in his direction." Looking at the silent dawn
I thought, "Alas Madhuban. Kunal, alas!"

I kept staring at the wine-colored stone in my ring which
glittered even in the half darkness. By concentrating on the
color I tried to still my mind. Then, suddenly, like insects flying
in through an open window, a few words heard long ago
flitted in and played inside my mind. At first I didn't know
what these words meant and where they'd come from. After a
few moments I realized they were words of a prayer I'd learnt
in my boyhood. I laughed as I remembered these forgotten
words. As I played with them in my mind I also recalled how
I'd learnt to meditate in my adolescence. I used to stare at the
picture of a black and white wheel; when I closed my eyes
after some time, the wheel would seem to come directly at me,
exactly between my eyebrows where the nose begins, the point
which is called *agya-chakra*. I had learnt a lot of these things.

After my initiation as a Brahman I had to learn all the traditional rituals of worship and prayer. I remember that during
the first few days after the sacred thread ceremony when I had
to stay in a closed room and observe certain rules very strictly,
I had stolen sweets. I also vividly remembered one very cold
morning when I was going to the Brahmaputra with my cousin
Taraprasad to immerse my ochre bag, tied on the top of a
stick, a last ritual which concluded my initiation as a Brahman.
Taraprasad stood above me in his shorts, on the high banks of
the river and yawned. I looked up at him once and then ran
down the slope to the water. My steps dislodged a lump of
earth and it slid into the river very softly. My ochre bag and stick
floated away on the muddy surface of the water. Standing in
the river with the water up to my waist I watched them recede.
The sky was pale blue, but everything else was ochre, the color
of soft earth. Everything around me was serene and detached,
and there was a touch of blue mist in the air. Soft waves broke
on the bank and the slow current bore away my ochre bag
and stick, still not too far away. They looked strange, as if the
clothes of a drowning hermit were floating away. It seemed to
me that perhaps the solution to the mystery of life and death
lay only a few steps ahead. Just a few steps ahead. The faded
earth-colored water and land around me spread out their hands
like an ascetic begging me as a gift. They wanted me to accompany my discarded bag and stick as far as I could. I wondered
why I should ever go back. Taraprasad dragged me home after
I'd stood in the water for a long time without any consciousness
of time. I moved about in a daze for many days afterwards.

    This morning it all came back to me. I did my best to divert
my mind. I played with the words of the forgotten prayer and
tried to concentrate by looking at the stone on my ring. After
many years my adolescent urge to renounce the world had taken
possession of me.

    Kunal will never know that I have renounced this world
more than he has. When I was going to the office, Sona re-
minded me that it was our wedding anniversary. I'd quite forgotten. Four years had passed. I am thirty-six now and Sona

must be twenty-eight. From the foot of the stairs I looked up towards her and smiled when our eyes met, the familiar smile of understanding each other. When I stepped outside, the busy hot streets of Calcutta made me feel normal again. I was ashamed to think that an anonymous letter had the power to make me stay away from work yesterday.

My office is in Middleton Street. At the door the old watchman left his stool and stood up respectfully. The lively girl at the reception counter nodded with a smile. "Morning sir," a junior officer greeted me as he crossed the hall. I did not use the lift. After a long time I felt very light and easy today. My footsteps resounded as I jumped several steps at a time and climbed the four flights of stairs. A continuous sound of typing came from the room of the typist. My personal stenographer was waiting outside my small office room. I smiled at the efficient young man and entered my air-conditioned little office. The table was covered with green glass, the cushion on my chair was deep and at my back, through a wide glass window, one could see the familiar scene of the maidan. I took off my jacket, put it on a hanger and opened the window. A cool breeze filled the room and with it came the mild smoky smell of burnt leaves. I absorbed the coolness, the smell, the sun and the air with all my being. I thought of my smug secure life. Only a few unfulfilled desires occasionally, and perhaps sometimes a little monotony; there was never any other serious trouble. 'I am happy,' I thought, and settled into my chair with a sigh.

In the afternoon Sona telephoned. I was startled to hear her voice suddenly. "What's happened?" I asked.

"Why, nothing." She laughed. "Do you remember, Raja, I asked you to bring some wool. I just wanted to remind you. I've put the sample in the right hand pocket of your jacket. I need four balls."

"I can't," I said. "This would mean running around the shops after office hours. Besides, it's too much bother finding the exact shade."

"But you must," Sona's voice came through with a smile. "If you don't bring it, who will? Who else do I have except you?"

I smiled, too. Sona knows exactly how to handle me. After
a brief pause she said, "Now, don't forget about this evening.
What is it? Let's see if you remember."

"Today?" I pretended to think. "Oh, it must be baby's birthday."

"You rogue," she said.

"But isn't it?"

"All right. It's baby's birthday. Only remember to come home
on time."

Then another silence. I knew she was still on the phone.
I hesitated to put it down. Suddenly she asked, "Raja, why were
you startled to hear my voice today?"

A little embarrassed, I said, "When?"

"Were you afraid?"

"Afraid of what?"

"How should I know? Maybe afraid of having your wife
and child kidnapped, or of a fire burning down your house.
There are so many things a man can be afraid of."

"You rogue." I put the receiver down.

It was true that I was afraid, though not in the way Sona
thought. It was a vague uneasy feeling.

After office hours I went around the shops selecting Sona's
wool very carefully and, as an anniversary present, bought a
cardigan for her, yellow and crimson embroidered on black,
then bought some flowers and a couple of Bengali novels. When
I stepped out of the bookshop, suddenly, for no reason, I felt
uneasy. Suppose Kunal sees me at this moment? Who knows,
he may be hiding in the crowd and watching his dear Madhuban:
Madhuban in an expensive suit, carrying a packet of wool, his
wife's cardigan wrapped in a piece of paper, and, in the other
hand, flowers and fiction. I do not know why I felt ashamed of
myself and tried to cover my face behind the spray of tuberoses.
The next moment my uneasiness passed—but I can't deny that
for a few seconds I was deeply disturbed.

That evening our party went off very well. My old friend
Atish had come with his wife, and there were some other
friends and relatives. When all the guests were leaving Atish

took me aside to the foot of the stairs and asked in a low voice, "What's happened? I heard you received an anonymous letter?"

I nodded. "But who told you?"

"Your wife!" he smiled. "She is scared out of her wits. She says you've changed since you received it. She says you've been crying."

"What rubbish!"

"Who wrote it?" Atish almost whispered.

"Kunal," I told him. "Kunal Mitra."

"I see." Atish tried to remember something. "Didn't he send you another letter about four years back?"

"Yes. Soon after I got married."

"What does Kunal say this time?"

"Many years ago I'd warned Kunal that the rebel's path turns back to domesticity. From the forest the ascetic returns home. He has sent those words back to me."

"He *is* trying to tease you," Atish smiled. I nodded. Atish sighed and said, "Poor thing, what more can he do?"

I looked at him, confused.

Atish smiled wanly, "Madhuban, I have been in touch with Kunal. I know he was working in a factory somewhere in a small town in Howrah district. He was in a miserable condition when I met him last year. I told him he should come to you. You have a good job; you might help him. But he refused. He asked me never to tell you about his condition. I had promised. Today I had to break my promise only to restore your peace of mind, Madhuban."

After a slight pause, Atish added, "Don't worry, Madhuban. He has nothing in his life now except these little tricks and surprises. He has a large family—a number of children—he does not have much time to bother about you. Yet he sends these letters to you occasionally just for a little fun."

Atish left after demolishing my image of Kunal completely. I came back to my room. Sona had put the baby to sleep and was standing in front of the dressing table mirror. She greeted me with a laugh: "How are you Mr. Ex-rebel and friend of Kunal Mitra? Perhaps you can smile at me now?"

I smiled. I knew Atish must have guessed the whole thing and told her about Kunal. Yet how could I explain to her that I was still not happy.

I didn't really care whether Kunal himself was still a rebel or not. It didn't matter to me whether he had come back to the world he had once renounced. I had moved away from his orbit of my own will. I have a quiet secure life now. Yet I like to think of one who had the courage to renounce the world. Not that I am interested in rebellion or politics. Now I love to hear the sound of a sewing machine, the cry of my little son, I love to look at dolls inside a glass case or flowers arranged in a vase. Only, in between these moments of happiness, I also like to think of my other self roaming around fields and forests, across farms and hills and mountains. That is why the news about Kunal did not surprise me pleasantly. I always knew that the path of the rebel would turn towards domesticity; from the forest the ascetic would return home. I always knew this.

At night Sona leaned over me and asked, "Are you un-happy?" I was surprised. "Why, no. Why should I be unhappy?"

"But I know you are."

"Why?"

"I don't know." She paused and then added. "I think some-times you want to give up all this and go away. You don't like this tame, purposeless life. I know."

"Don't be silly." I laughed loudly, but I could see that Sona's face had turned pale.

Just before she fell asleep, secure within my embrace, Sona said, "I am scared, Raja." Then the lizards within my heart started saying: don't go, don't go.

I pretended to be asleep by lying perfectly still. Then at midnight I got up to sit at my writing table and lit a small lamp. I must write a letter to Kunal. Not the Kunal I know— but a different man—a Kunal I shall never know.

All night long I wrote that letter. I smoked cigarette after cigarette, and then, towards dawn, I must have fallen asleep with my head on the table. Sona woke me in the morning. Her face was distorted with fear. Her lips trembled as she cried, "Raja, what have you been doing all night?" I smiled peacefully and indicated the letter. She did not know what I meant.

"I have been writing a letter, Sona, an anonymous letter," I explained.

"Oh, no," she exclaimed. "Why, it's only one sentence!"

She bent over my shoulder and read the letter aloud: "Kunal, the hermit at home is more disturbed than the ascetic abroad."

Translated from the Bengali by Meenakshi Mukherjee

The Corpse

JAGANNATH PRASAD DAS

Someone's lifeless body lies in the street
surrounded by people.
Many simply walk past,
others cannot bear to look at it;
one's step falters, another falls silent,
and another shuts his eyes at the sight.

One passes by reciting *mantras* along the street;
for whom did this child pluck flowers?
Who laughed here,
Who stretched out his arms
to put a halt to time,
and whose screams are lost
in the deserted street?

In the light's rush upstream,
someone was lost on the way; the heart's
many dreams were ground to ash.
Someone sighs deeply.
Someone measures out life
with a burning candle,
and another finds his own way
in the half-light.

The people have all gone;
the street is deserted, laughter extinguished
in the endlessness of space.
The corpse lies in the middle of the street.

And I lie fast asleep on a lonely isle.

Translated from the Oriya by Jayanta Mahapatra

Five Poems

JAYANTA MAHAPATRA

Total Solar Eclipse

February 16, 1980, Puri, India

It was the drawn-out cry of day
that left behind no echo,
day that became meek as a frightened child:
a banner of human skin
fluttered keenly on top of the temple of Jagannath.

From the maze of alleys
that lead down to the giant temple street
the souls of simpler men
groaned in the harsh voices of ash,
afraid to reveal their bodies,
peering here and there like hunted dogs.
Above was the pallid face of a corpse,
the wretched bowel of time:

emerging from the dark caves of space
the wind, the obsession, the nightmare,
to affirm only what these men would let come
through precious paschal fast, dire superstition.

Quietly the moon's dark well moved on,
against the stone pillars, the disturbed blood, the dust,
the pigments and embers, against the lonely foetus of Puri—
what use is there in this naked affirmation?
The cobra slides along the waiting hill
with its unveiled peril,
the hyena sniffs at the sudden cool air
and lets out a despairing wail
at its bewilderment of this new image of night.
Slowly the vultures turn away
from the warm belly of the sky,
recognizing the silence of the black wind
whose throat drips horizons of fire;
the sparrows converge upon the palpitating gulmohar,
leaves already seamed for sleep.

And cautiously, the crocodile
pushes its long snout out of the deep water
like the fearsome Brahmin priest in the temple,
secure by shadowy layers of sleep,
so out of date, in alleviative belief,
using the darkness to be a portent of the gods
who had merely revealed a last occasion
to hide the disrobing of human values
                                        by a rabid civilization.

Sarita

A kestrel sits heavily on a mango bough in the yard.
Its ash-grey wings closed to preying silence. And my house
of wind as though lost in its way in the sun.

A lizard slithers by on the ground. The slow voice
of God calls people from the lime-washed mosque.
The girl of the brothel to whom I made love last night

sleeps curled up under the day's warm hill.
But my wounds have opened again this morning.
Behind the dark cupboard a fleshless rat peers out at the light.

In the empty stadium by the river a rich boy
practices in full track suit. Chants thread the light of dawn.
He thinks of his dream girl Sarita sleeping with someone

in some hotel room in Bangkok and runs faster.
I look at my unwashed face in a palmful of water.
The slum water at a lonely well twitches

convulsively in its own darkness.
Another light, buried and pale, grows in my eyes.
I see the kestrel fly off, the prey wriggling in the air.

The Vase

The strong south wind hits our faces again,
it's October;
sunsets are fiery red
and the waters of wells are clear already—
there we are, under the mango tree,
in the old house, amid the drift of things,
the vase on the bookcase with shadows of swifts
    reeling around it,
and we don't know whether we are alone any more.
But each day we watch the swifts come and go,
watch the still-slender, teasing whore
who shuffles down the crowded road and finds out
that the middle-aged man surreptitiously following her
is only listening to the slowing sounds of his own heart;
and we sit and long for the child who left in seventythree,
and behave like our bitch that catches a scent
    and sniffs about in the air.
We look around today and the day after tomorrow,
remembering those who caught us like irrigation-canals
across the dry nights in the distant countryside,
and remembering suddenly, someone
who once envied us and our bodies,
    so impudent, glistening with rain.
Ah, this voice I hear now,
what answer do I owe you?
The tree trembles in the wind,
the house where we once made love
now weakens at the knees. And all the time
that gathered into those moments
fills the grave of the vast vase with dust.

An Indian Journal

What's in my father's house
is not mine. In his eyes,

dirty and thick as rainwater
flowing into earth, is the ridicule

my indifference quietly left behind:
the sun has imperceptibly withdrawn,

and nothing stirs there
except for two discolored kites

and the whisper of an old myth in the clouds.
Thinking to escape his beliefs,

I go to meet the spectre of belief,
a looming shadow the color of mud

watery and immense as the Gangā.
It's thus how men are made,

and my father's father, so very dead,
can no more will my father

the despair that drags him from sleep
rotten with rust, with all gloss gone:

I have taken my likeness down
from his walls and hidden it

in the river's roots: a colorless monsoon
eaten away by what has drifted between us.

An Impotent Poem

The dust settles in the creases of my skin.
The sun floods the trees, the sweet sweat smell
of a woman walking quietly by

with a market basket of bananas on her head.
The slender neck, the earth-color of her throat;
and in the shadows of mine, my words merely
draw up over the land, they aren't humble words
anymore. My body, left behind,
a night glow on the window,
filling the rural moments with protective gesture.
Seeing you in the dark, where knives flash,
as the mind comes out of the void to get you.
Now the heart says: You must find a new way,
try to turn the desire you hold into fierce power.
I watch the sun move on, rustle the leaves
as a fog of crow calls covers the town, the torn mat
on the entrance floor, and the dead face
of the secret war I thought had to be won
sags as my body turns away from yours heavy with scorn.

The Recluse

MANOHAR SHETTY

Phantoms roaming in his head
He wakes every morning from the spell of the dead.
Mucous lids dense as cobwebs
Inspect a wall, a bewildered bed.

The air crackles and hums like cables,
Newspapers drop like bombs on doorsteps:
No one disturbs him who traces
The shreds of light on the ceiling.

But tense as the lizard on his window-sill,
He cocks his ears to a train's whistle
Fading into sun-stroked hills,
Immense in their lonely will.

Five Poems

AGYEYA

Concerning Love

Here on the isles of Hellas
We love our wives
And wish they were somehow
Different from what they are.

There in Egypt
They don't love whores
But like them always to remain
What they are.

The Dissenter

They kept nodding 'yes,' 'yes,'
And the garlands
Piled higher round their necks.
They moved smoothly
Through carpeted tunnels of bunting.

May they have the joy
Of their assenting.

But may he too
For whom dissent
Is destiny,
Whenever called
Stand up without qualm,
Without regret,
And answer, 'No!'
Broken on the rock of history
May he yet with unruffled calm
Call 'No!'

Heroes

Hooded head and shoulders
They kept repeating
They would never show their backs:
And we kept cheering them on.

But as they fell
And their visors turned over
We saw they had no faces.

Friendship

I had asked then:
Among the *rasas*
Is there a *rasa* of friendship?

And today you said:
This meeting after years . . .
How sad!
It is the same love as always
But is there any name for this new pain?

June Night

The river, a gorged python,
Worms into the shadow
Of the sagging cliff;
The moon is pale with the breathless heat.
The road winds interminably.

Nightjars rasp as tireless cicadas rewind
Their clocks
Timing a weary pair of oxen panting
Before a load that was the same
Forty centuries ago.

An unbreathable vacancy has dominion.
There is no privacy anywhere, no silence.

Translated from the Hindi by the author

Three Poems

G. S. SHARAT CHANDRA

At The India Association

Greetings.
I'm so glad to see so many of you have come
for this function on our independence day.
The elections were held as we said in our notice
but nobody showed up
& I was elected President.
Let me introduce you to all our past Presidents
who are standing beside the foosball machine.
Give them a hand.
Next on our agenda is refreshments.
I'm told the pizzas have arrived.
I'm sorry we are serving American food
on Indian Independence but our women are too busy
to cook independently because of children.
First, the children will form a line,
afterwards, the ladies can proceed,
then it will be the chance for men.
One piece only per person, thank you.
Now, I'm asking Miss Prakash to give us a song
but before she begins to sing
I have a few words about our 34th independence day.
Mahatma Gandhi, Jawaharlal Nehru, Rajgopalachari,
the list goes on & on,
have proved that might is not always right.
Our children should know this
so far away from our leaders.
Is there anybody else who wants to say
a few words about our independence?
After Miss Prakash, there will be singing of many hits
by Ghose, Bhose & Bhatt.
Anybody else who wants to sing any other song is welcome.
Even if the function comes to an end after singing
I hope to meet one and all to chat.
Lastly in the name of our country,
please remember to pay all your dues

& attend all elections.
Who knows somewhere right here in this group
might be sitting the President of our next year's election!
Come low wind or high water in our politics,
may we all have jolly good time today.

Facts of Life

My father, teetotaler, vegetarian,
took two baths a day,
one at dawn the other
before his evening obeisance
to lord Shiva at the temple.

Cleanliness of forms,
the given and the gifted,
adherence to principles,
honesty, truth, purity,
were things he'd die for.

Yet he died of a malignancy
whose virtue was pillage,
whose form spread
from viscera to vision,
from body to soul.

Now he who loved roses
lies buried within the limits
of his caste's cemetery
by the river Kabini
where the banyans sway,

where transients and pilgrims
come to celebrate Shiva's victory
over one demon or another,
seek its tall crabgrass
their revelries to defecate.

A Quick Glimpse of Buddha's Children On The American TV Between Its Commercials

Kampuchean boy
after his daily breakfast
of Thai wind, ricemud, raindust,
covers his nose from his sister
who sleeps through it—
She chose to breed flies in her eyes,
nostrils, in her sweet red mouth.
He can already see her
in Buddha's heaven
rainbows in her wings.

The Moon

DINA NATH NADIM

The moon looked like a pancake as she rose
behind the hills. She looked dull as a robe
of pampore tweed worn off threadbare and torn
at the collar-band out of which peep the scars
on a marble breast, and pale as a counterfeit
silver coin which robs a coolie of her mite.
                 The moon looked like a pancake and
the hills looked hungry; and the clouds put out
the fire in western skies. But in the east
the wood nymphs lit the moon's cooking stove
in whose soft glow shoots of the steaming rice
seemed to spring upon the hills. I whispered
hope to my hungry belly, and gazed and gazed,
with hungry looks, at the moon-flooded sky.

Translated from the Kashmiri by J. L. Kaul

Two Poems

KESHAV MALIK

In Praise of Guns

The clouds burst in praise of guns,
Especially when Cains rehearse
The ancient curse.

Then trumpeters trumpet the hearse
Of each brave son—
Circumcised and non.

God in heaven, who pour out in such fun,
When scorn answers in cold coin of scorn
Tooth for tooth, eye for eye.

From age to age so the show goes on—
The soul's gaze fixed
On mirroring pools of blood.

The clouds burst in praise of guns
In praise of sons—
A red thread running through a hole in lungs.

Lightning and thunder commend violence,
The charioteer winks approval, let
Shot answer shot.

The Date

Where would you like to meet her?
Suddenly, under the smooth hypnotic wheels
Upon the elegant highway! Or
Would you rather care to greet her
Accidentally, head on, by the swaying necklace
Of the well-lit bay. Perhaps
You will neck her by night
In the slim streets of the beloved

Medieval town!—prefer to be surprised
With mysterious sensations upon your crown?
Oh, of course; for being now in close embrace
Upon the four poster is out of fashion;
No, one is no longer so impassioned,
Date her outdoors (waiting for years
On end not such fun), meet her casually, on the sly.
Hi sister!—
Cheat her boldly,
Really, she's a sport and so spontaneous.

An Indian Dog Show

SISIR KUMAR DAS

I never knew this city
had so many dogs,
lovely and ugly and crooked,
fierce and temerarious and intemperate,
some almost resembling intellectuals,
without a sense of humor;
          dogs so different
          in colors and calls,
          callings and manners,
          forms and shapes,
          and in their world-views,
          and in the views of the world.
Yet what a wonder—
All of them understand and
understand and obey
the English language.

Translated from the Bengali by the author

At Bus-Stop

ARUN SEDWAL

She gives me
a scorpion look
before parting with
a blank suburban smile
while I look over her shoulders
at the evening newspaper

STERILIZATION FOR RATS
MADE COMPULSORY

Her blood-colored nails
turn the page

RURAL BIAS URGED IN KITE-FLYING

Together we wait for
the bus

SUICIDE BY KILLER

A silk-cotton seed settles
in her ruffled hair
smelling of coconut oil
a birthmark on her cheeks
like a miniature map of Japan

PURSE-SNATCHERS AT LARGE

Few winks in her eyes
few steps forward
whir of an auto-rickshaw
a trail of nasty exhaust

I look around and feel for my purse
there is nobody except
a lone crow pecking at
the bus-stop sign.

Two Poems

SOUBHAGAYA KUMAR MISRA

Robinson Crusoe

The far, far sea (its waters blue and cool)
cast me mercifully on this isle,
gave me supplies from the wrecked boat
and said: build your home and live here.

But where is my home? And is anything here?
Uneven rock, bramble and shrub, gray sands,
no path to walk on, not a single companion
to talk to, no food; how can I live here?

Not a single tree, no shade, just the fiery sun;
a handful of dry leaves blow
                              in the wind
and join to the present those tender green memories:
here too there once were trees, and life, and flowers in bloom.

The old tobacco is stale;
not a single shoot grows from the barley I sow;
deprived of rain, the cracked salty earth
bares its huge teeth and mocks my efforts.

I accept silence here as law.
How helpless I am in this merciless prison!
Rocks lie about aimlessly;
the fatted sheep of my patience is sacrificed here.

No one pays heed to my: "Brother, just a moment"
as I walk the tarred road of this town;
I feel homeless as Robinson Crusoe,
thrown on a deserted isle by fate.

And I watch cruel savages
tear and gnaw each other's flesh and bone.
We gorge ourselves on meat and warm, raw blood;
why, then, this chant of glory, why this pious Thursday?

Translated from the Oriya by Jayanta Mahapatra

The Hill

Who is that man, the one
who has already climbed
onto the top of the bare hill
so early in the morning?
Why is he standing there?
If the hill were to vanish for a moment
he would look like a picture
hung from the sky
above the herd of cattle
and the banyan tree.
He looks like a man
determined to be hanged,
waiting for a rope.

People go up to a certain height
whenever they need to find
someone, something:
lost cattle or the convict
who escaped by jumping a wall,
the son who left in anger,
without his food.
The man is standing still
as if to find everything
for everybody,
once and for all, by gazing
off the hill
into the valley,
toward the high tide
at sea, toward the secret
congregation of enemies.

Suddenly he stirs.
The water of the sky stirs too.
He raises his hand and knocks
on an invisible door;
then he throws challenges at air.
Birds scatter in all directions;
the cattle run helter-skelter;
the tree's shade breaks like glass;

the blood of his relatives
turns watery pale.
After cuckoos have laid their eggs,
secretly in the crows' nests;
after the bangles have been removed
from the bride's wrists,
he lies flat and clutches the earth
on the bare hilltop, his arms
outstretched, demanding
nothing less than intimacy,
as if he'll lose himself,
now that it's time.

We will certainly go to find him.
We are his friends,
relatives, neighbors, supposed
to stand by his side
at the king's door and
at his cremation ground.
If to our bad luck we don't find him
we will have his image carved,
placed on top of the hill.
For a long time we'll live
with our doubts, pass
and repass the place that was his.

Translated from the Oriya by the author

A Bride for the Sahib

KHUSHWANT SINGH

"What can I do for you, gentlemen?"

Mr. Sen asked the question without looking up. He pushed the cleaner through the stem of his pipe and twirled it round. As he blew through it, his eye fell on the rose and marigold garlands in the hands of his callers. So they knew that he had been married that morning! He had tried to keep it as quiet as possible. But as he had learned so often before, it was impossible to keep anything a secret for too long in his nosey native land.

He screwed on the bowl to the stem and blew through the pipe again. Through his lowered eyes, he saw his visitors shuffling their feet and nudging each other. He unwrapped his plastic tobacco pouch and began filling his pipe. After an uneasy minute of subdued whispers, one of the men cleared his throat.

"Well, Mr. Bannerjee, what is your problem?" asked Mr. Sen in a flat monotone.

"Saar," began the Superintendent of the clerical staff, "Whee came to wheesh your good shelph long liphe and happinesh." He beckoned to the Chaprasis: "Garland the Sahib."

The Chaprasis stepped in front with the garlands held aloft. The Sahib stopped them with a wave of his pipe. "*Mez par*—on the table," he commanded in his gentle but firm voice. The Chaprasis' hands came down slowly; their fawning smiles changed to stupid grins. They put the garlands on the table and stepped behind the semi-circle of clerks.

"If that is all," said Mr. Sen, standing up, "we can get back to our work. I thank you, gentlemen, for your good wishes." He bowed slightly to indicate that they should leave. "Bannerjee, will you look in later to discuss the redistribution of work while I am away?"

"Shuttenly, Saar."

The men joined the palms of their hands, murmured their "namastes" and filed out.

Sen joined his hands across the waist-coat and watched the smoke from his pipe rise in a lazy spiral towards the ceiling. A new chapter in his life had begun. That's how Hindus described marriage—the third of the four stages of life according to the Vedas. It was alarming, he reflected, how his thought processes slipped into clichés and how Hinduism extended its tentacles in practically every sphere of life. His father had not been a particularly orthodox Hindu and had sent him to an Anglo-Indian School where the boys had changed his name from Santosh to Sunny. Thereafter he had gone to Balliol. He had entered the Administrative Service before the Independent Indian Government with its new-fangled nationalist ideas had made Hindi and a vernacular language compulsory. His inability to speak an Indian language hadn't proved a handicap. As a matter of fact, it impressed most Indians. Although his accent and mannerism made him somewhat of an outsider, it was more than compensated by the fact that it also put him outside the vicious circle of envy and back-biting in which all the others indulged. They sought his company because he was an un-Indian Indian, because he was a brown British gentleman, because he was what the English contemptuously described as a Wog—a westernized oriental gentleman.

Sen's main contact with his country was his mother. Like an orthodox Hindu widow she shaved her head, only wore a plain white sari and went in bare feet. He was her only child so they both did the best they could for each other. She ran his home. He occasionally ate rice, curried fish and sticky over-sweetened confections she made on special occasions. Other times she had the bearer cook him the lamb chops and the shepherd pies he liked better. She had converted one of the rooms to a temple where she burnt incense and tinkled bells to a diminutive image of the black-faced, red-tongued goddess,

Kali. But she never insisted on his joining her in worship. Although he detested Indian movies, he made it a point to take her to one every month. She, at her end, did not object to his taking his evening Scotch and soda or smoking in her presence. She never questioned him about his movements. They got on extremely well till she started talking about his getting married. At first he had laughed it off. She became insistent and started to nag him. She wanted to see him properly settled. She wanted to fondle a grandson just once before she died, she said with tears in her eyes. At last he gave in. He did not have strong views on marriage or on whom he would marry. Since he had come back to settle in India, he could not do worse than marry one of his countrywomen. "Alright Ma, you find me a wife. I'll marry anyone you want me to marry," he said one day.

His mother did not bring up the subject again for many days. She wrote to her brother living at Dehra Dun, in the Himalayan foothills, to come down to Delhi. The two drafted an advertisement for the matrimonial columns and asked for insertions in two successive Sunday editions of the *Hindustan Times*. It read: "Wanted a fair, good-looking virgin of a high class respectable family for an Oxford-educated Bengali youth of 25, drawing over Rs. 1,000 p.m., in first class gazetted Government Service. Applicant should be coversant with H.H. affairs. C and D no bar. Correspond with horoscope. P.O. Box No. 4200."

The first insertion brought over fifty letters from parents who enclosed not only the horoscopes of their daughters but their photographs as well to prove that they were fair and therefore good-looking. A fortnight later the applications were sorted out and Sunny's mother and uncle triumphantly laid out nearly a hundred photographs on the large dining table. Their virginity and capacity to deal with household affairs had, of necessity, to be taken on trust. But despite the professed indifference to the C and D, the applicants selected for consideration were of the same caste as the Sens and whose fathers had made offers of substantial dowries. Now it was for Sunny to choose.

This was the first time that Sunny had heard of the matrimonial advertisement. He was very angry and acutely embarrassed as some anxious parents had travelled up all the way

from Calcutta, bribed the clerks concerned at the newspaper
office and called on him at the office. He told his mother
firmly that if it did not stop, he would call off the whole thing.
But as he had given his word, he would accept anyone chosen
for him. His mother and uncle quickly settled the matter by
selecting a girl whose father promised the largest dowry and
gave a substantial portion of it as earnest money at the betrothal
ceremony. The parties took the horoscopes of the affianced couple to a Pandit who consulted the stars and, having had his palm
crossed with silver, pronounced the pair ideally suited to each
other and the dates that suited the parties to be most auspicious.
That was as much as Sunny Sen could take. He told them quite
bluntly that he would be married at the Registry or not at all.
His mother and uncle sensed his mounting irritation and gave
in. The bride's parents made a nominal protest: the cost of a
wedding on the tradition pattern, which included feasting the
bride-groom's party and relations, giving of presents and paying
the priests, could run into thousands of rupees. The registrar's
fee was only Rs. 5.00. That was how Srijut Santosh Sen came
to marry Kumari Kalyani, the eldest of Srijut Profulla and
Srimati Protima Das's five daughters. Mr. Das was, like his
son-in-law, a first class gazetted Government servant.

The honeymoon also created difficulties. His mother blushed
as if he had said something improper. The Das's were outraged
at the suggestion that their daughter should go away for a
fortnight unaccompanied by a younger sister. But they resigned
their daughter to her fate. Her husband had been brought up
as a Sahib and she must follow his ways.

Sen's thoughts were interrupted by his colleague Santa Singh
bursting into the room. The Sikh was like the rest of his race,
loud and aggressive: "Brother, you think you can run away
without giving us a party?" he yelled as he came. "We insist on
having feast to welcome our sister-in-law."

Sen stood up quickly and put his hand across the table to
keep the Sikh at an arm's length. Santa Singh ignored the
proffered hand, came round the table and enveloped his friend
in his arms. He planted his wet and hirsute kisses on the Sahib's
cheeks. "Congratulations, brother, when are we to meet our
sister-in-law?"

"Soon, very soon," replied Sen, extricating himself from the Sikh's embrace and wiping his cheeks. And before the words were out of his mouth, he knew he had blundered: "As soon as we get back from our honeymoon."

"Honeymoon!" exclaimed Santa Singh with a leer; he took Sen's hands in his and squeezed them amorously. "I hope you've had yourself massaged with chamelion oil; puts more punch into things. You should also add crushed almonds in your milk. Above all, don't overdo it. Not more than . . . . " There was no stopping the Sikh from giving unsolicited advice on how to approach an inexperienced virgin and the proper use of aphrodisiacs. Sen kept smiling politely without making comment. When he had enough, he interrupted the Sikh's soliloquy by extending his hand. "It was very kind of you to have dropped in. We will call on you and Mrs. Singh as soon as we are back in Delhi."

Santa Singh took Sen's hand without any enthusiasm. "Good-bye. Have a nice time," he blurted and went out. Sen sat down with a sigh of relief. He knew he had not been rude. He had behaved with absolute rectitude—exactly like an English gentleman.

A minute later the Chaprasi raised the thick curtains to let in Mr. Swami, the Director of the Department. Sen again extended his hand across the table to keep the visitor at arm's length: the native's desire to make physical contact galled him. "Good morning, Sir."

The Director touched Sen's hand with his without answering the greeting. His mouth was full of betel saliva. He raised his face to hold it from dribbling out and bawled out to the Chaprasi: "Hey, spitton *lao*."

The Chaprasi ran in with the vessel which Sen had ordered to be removed from his room and held it under the Director's chin. Mr. Swami spat out the bloody phlegm in the spittoon. Sen opened his table drawer and pretended he was looking for his match box. The Director sat down and lit his bidi. "Eh, you Sen, you are a dark harse. By God, a pitch black harse, if I may say so." Mr. Swami fancied his knowledge of English idiom. "So quietly you go and get yourself hitched. My steno says 'Sir, we should celebrate holiday to celebrate Sahib's marriage!' I say,

'What marriage, man?' 'Sir, Mr. Sen got married this morning.'
'By God,' I said, 'I must get the truth, the whole truth and
nothing but the truth right from the harse's mouth—the dark
harse's mouth.' " The Director stretched his hand across the table.
"Clever guy you, eh?" he said with a smirk. Sen touched his
boss's hand with the tip of his fingers. "Thank you, Sir."

"What for thank you? And you come to the office on the
day you get married. Heavens won't fall if you stay away a
few days. I as your boss order you to go back home to your wife.
I will put in a demi-official memo. What do you say?"

The Director was pleased with himself and extended his
hand. Sen acknowledged his boss's wit by taking his hand.
"Thank you, Sir. I think I will go home."

"My God, you are a Sahib! I hope your wife is not a Mem
Sahib. That would be too much of a joke."

The Director left but his betel-stained smirk lingered on like
the smile of the Cheshire Cat and his last remark began to go
round and round in Sen's head with an insistent rhythmic beat.
"I hope your wife isn't a Mem Sahib, not a Mem Sahib, not a
Mem Sahib. I hope your wife is not a Mem Sahib."

Would his wife be a Mem Sahib, he mused as he drove
back home for lunch. It was not very likely. She claimed to be
an M.A. in English Literature. But he had met so many of his
countrymen with long strings of firsts who could barely speak
the English language correctly. To start with, there was the
Director himself with his "okey dokes" and "by gums" who,
like other South Indians, pronounced eight as 'yate,' an egg as
a 'yugg,' and who always stumbled on words beginning with an
'M.' He smiled to himself as he recalled the Director instructing
his private secretary to get Mr. M. M. Amir, Member of Parlia-
ment, on the phone. "I want Yum Yum Yumeer, Yumpee." The
Bengalis had their own execrable accent: they added an airy
'h' whenever they could after a 'b' or a 'w' or an 's.' A "virgin"
sounded like some exotic tropical plant, the "vharjeen," "will"
as a "wheel," and the "simple" as a "shimple." There was much
crying at the farewell and the bride continued to sniffle for a
long time afterwards in the car. She had drawn her sari over
her forehead down to her eyes and covered the rest of her face

with a silk handkerchief into which she blew her nose. When Sen lit his pipe, she firmly clamped the handkerchief on her nostrils. "Does the smoke bother you?" was the first sentence he spoke to his wife. She replied by a vigorous shake of the head.

They stopped at a mango orchard by the roadside to have lunch. His mother had made two separate packets with their names in Bengali pinned on them. The one marked 'Sunny' had roasted chicken and cheese sandwiches. The other contained boiled rice and pickles in a small brass cup with curried lentils. His wife poured the lentils on the rice and began to eat with her fingers.

They ate without speaking to each other. Within a few minutes they had an audience of anxious passers-by and children from a neighboring village. Some sat on their haunches; others just stood gaping at the couple or commenting on their being newly married. Sen knew how to deal with the rustic. "Are you people hungry?" he asked sarcastically.

The men turned away sheepishly; but the urchins did not budge. "Bugger off, you dirty bastards," roared Sen, raising his hand as if to strike. The children ran away to a safe distance and began to yell back at Sen, mimicking his English. "Buggeroff, Buggeroff," they cried. "Arey he is a Sahib, a big Sahib."

Sen ignored them and spoke politely to his wife. "Pardon the language," he said with a smile. "Would you like to sample one of my sandwiches? I don't know whether you eat meat; take the lettuce and cheese; it is fresh cheddar."

Mrs. Sen took the sandwich with her curry-stained fingers. She tore a strip off the toast as if it were a Chapati, scooped up a mixture of rice, curry and cheddar and put it in her mouth. She took one bite and stopped munching. Through her thick glasses she stared at her husband as if he had given her poison. She turned pale and being unable to control herself any further, spat out the food in her mouth. She turned her face the other way and brought up the rice and curry.

"I am dreadfully sorry," stammered Sen. "The cheddar upset you. I should have known."

Mrs. Sen wiped her mouth with the end of her sari and asked for water. She rinsed her mouth and splashed it on her

face. The lunch was ruined. "We better be on our way," said
Sen, standing up. "That is if you feel better."

She tied up her brass cup in a duster and followed him to the
car. They were on the road again. She fished out a silver box
from her handbag and took out a couple of betel leaves. She
smeared one with lime and catechu paste, put in cardamom and
sliced betel nuts, rolled it up and held it out for her husband.

"I'm afraid I don't touch the stuff," he said apologetically.
"I'll stick to my pipe if you don't mind." Mrs. Sen did not mind.
She slipped the leaf in her own mouth and began to chew con-
tentedly.

They got to the rest-house in good time. The rest-house bearer
took in the luggage and spread the bedding rolls. He asked Mrs.
Sen what they would like for dinner. She referred him to her
husband. "Just anything for me," he replied, "omelette or anything. Ask the Mem Sahib what she would like for herself. I
will take a short walk before dinner."

"Don't go too far, Sahib," continued the bearer. "This is
wild country. There is a foot-path down the river which the
Sahibs who come to fish take. It is quite safe."

Sen went into the bedroom to ask his wife if she would like
to come out for a walk. She was unpacking her things. He
changed his mind. "I'll go for a short stroll towards the river.
Get the bearer to put out the Scotch and soda in the verandah;
there's a bottle in my suitcase. We'll have a drink before dinner."

His wife nodded her head.

The well-beaten fishermen's footpath snaked its way through
a dense foliage of sal and flame of the forest, ending abruptly on
the pebbly bank of the river. The Ganges was a magnificent
sight; a broad and swift-moving current of clear, icy-blue water
sparkling in the bright sun. It must have been from places like
where he stood, he thought, that the sages of olden times had
pronounced the Ganges the holiest of all the rivers in the world.
He felt a sense of kinship with his Aryan ancestors, who worshipped the beautiful in nature, sang hymns to the rising sun,
raised goblets of fermented soma juice to the full moon and
who ate beef and were lusty with full-bosomed and large-
hipped women. Much water had flowed down the Ganges since

then and Hinduism was now like the river itself at its lower reaches—as at Calcutta where he was born. At Calcutta it was a sluggish expanse of slime and sludge, carrying the excrement of millions of pilgrims who polluted it at Hardwar, Benares, Allahabad, Patna and other "holy" cities on its banks, and who fouled its water by strewing charred corpses for the fish and the turtles to eat. It had become the Hinduism of the cow-protectors, prohibitionists—and chewers of betel leaves. That must be it, he thought cheerfully. His was the pristine Hinduism of the stream that sparkled before him; that of the majority, of the river after it, had been sullied by centuries of narrow prejudices. He walked over the pebbled bank, took up a palmful of the icy-cold water and splashed it on his face.

The shadows of the jungle lengthened across the stream and the cicadas began to call. Sen turned back and quickly retraced his steps to the bungalow. The sun was setting. It was time for a sundowner.

Tumblers and soda were laid out on the table in the verandah. The bearer heard his footsteps and came with a bunch of keys in his open hand. "I did not like to open the Sahib's trunk," he explained. "Please take out the whisky."

"Why didn't you ask the Mem Sahib to take it out?"

The bearer looked down at his feet. "She said she could not touch a bottle of alcohol. She gave me the keys but I don't like to meddle with the Sahib's luggage. If things are misplaced . . . "

"That's alright. Open my suitcase. The bottles of whisky and brandy are right on the top. And serve the dinner as soon as the Mem Sahib is ready."

It was no point asking his wife to sit with him. He poured himself a large Scotch and lit his pipe. Once more his thoughts turned to the strange course his life had taken. If he had married one of the English girls he had met in his University days how different things would have been. They would have kissed a hundred times between the wedding and the wedding night; they would have walked hand-in-hand through the forest and made love beside the river; they would have lain in each other's arms and sipped their Scotch. They would have nibbled at knick-knacks in between bouts of love; and they would have made love till the early hours of the morning. The whisky warmed his blood and quickened his imagination. He was back in England. The gathering bloom and the dark, tropical forest, accentuated the feeling of loneliness. He felt an utter stranger in his own country. He did not hear the bearer announcing that dinner had been served. Now his wife came out and asked in her quaint Bengali accent, "Do you want to shit outside?"

"What?" he asked gruffly, waking up from his reverie.

"Do you want to shit inshide or outshide? The deener ees on the table."

"Oh, I'll be right in. You go ahead. I'll join you in a second." Good lord! What would his English friends have said if she had invited them in this manner! The invitation to defecate was Mrs. Sen's first communication with her husband.

A strong sweet smell of coconut oil and roses assailed Sen's nostrils as he entered the dining room. His wife had washed and oiled her hair; it hung in loose snaky coils below her waist. The parting was daubed with bright vermilion powder to indicate her status as a married woman. He had no doubt that she had smeared her body with the attar of roses as her mother had probably instructed. She sat patiently at the table; being a Hindu woman, she could not very well start eating before her husband.

"Sorry to keep you waiting. You should have started. Your dinner must be cold."

She simply wagged her head.

They began to eat: his omelette and buttered slice of bread with his fork and knife; she, her rice and lentil curry mushed in between her fingers and palm of her right hand. Sen cleared his throat many times to start a conversation. But each time the vacant and bewildered look behind the thick lenses of his wife's glasses made him feel that words would fail to convey their meaning. If his friends knew they would certainly have a big laugh. "Oh Sunny Sen! How could he start talking to his wife? He hadn't been properly introduced. Don't you know he is an Englishman?"

The dinner was eaten in silence. Kalyani Sen emitted a soft belch and took out her betel-leaf case. She rolled a leaf, paused for a split-second and put it in her mouth. Sunny had promised himself the luxury of expensive Havana cigars over his honeymoon. He took one out of its phallic metal case, punctured its bottom with a gold clipper and lit it. The aromatic smoke soon filled the dining room. This time his wife did not draw the fold of her sari across her face; she simply clasped her hands in front of her mouth and discreetly blocked her nostrils with the back of her hands.

They sat in silence facing each other across the table; she chewing her leaf—almost like a cow chewing the cud, thought Sen. He, lost in the smoke of his long Cuban cigar. It was oppressive—and the barrier between them, impassable. Sen glanced at his watch and stood up. "News," he exclaimed loudly. "Mustn't miss the news." He went into the bedroom to fetch his transistor radio set.

Two beds had been laid side by side with no space between them; the pillows almost hugged each other. The sheets had been sprinkled with the earthy perfume of khas fibre and looked as if they also awaited the consummation of the marriage performed earlier in the day. How, thought Sen, could she think of this sort of thing when (they hadn't even been introduced! No, hell) barely a civil word had passed between them? He quickly took out his radio set and hurried back to the dining room.

He tuned in to Delhi. While he listened in to the news, the bearer cleared the table and left salaaming, "Good night, Sir." Mrs. Sen got up, collected her betel-leaf case and disappeared into the bedroom.

The fifteen minutes of news was followed by a commentary on sports. Sen had never bothered to listen in to it. He was glad he did because the commentary was followed by the announcement of a change in the program. A concert of vocal Hindustani music by Ustad Bade Ghulam Ali Khan had been put off to relay a performance by the Czech Philharmonic Orchestra from New Delhi. Ghulam Ali Khan was the biggest name in Indian music and even the Anglicized natives had to pretend that they admired the cacophony of gargling sounds he produced from the pit of his stomach. Members of the diplomatic corps were known to sit through four hours of the maestro's performance lest they offend their Indian hosts or be found less cultured than staffs of rival embassies. The Czech Philharmonic had come to India for the first time and the wogs who ran Delhi's European Music Society had got away with it. Pity, thought Sen, he wasn't in town; he could have invited the right people for dinner (tails, of course!) followed by the concert. How would his wife have fitted in a party of this sort?

The sound of applause came over the air, followed by an announcement that the opening piece was a selection from Smetana's "The Bartered Bride." Sen was transported back to the glorious evening at Covent Garden and the Festival Hall. Smetana was followed by Bartok. The only thing that broke the enchantment was the applause between the movements. How could one expect the poor, benighted natives to know that the end of a movement was not the end of the symphony!

There was an interval of ten minutes. The last piece was Sen's favorite-Dvorak's Symphony No. 5 in E minor. He poured himself a liquor brandy (V.S.O.P.), drew a chair and stretched his legs on it. He had never heard Dvorak as well performed even in Europe. A Cuban cigar, an excellent Cognac and the world's greatest music, what more could one ask for! He gently decapitated the cigar of its ashy head, lay back in the arm-chair and closed his eyes in complete rapture. By the final movement he was fast asleep with the cigar slowly burning itself out between his lips.

Neither the applause, at the end of the concert, nor the silence and the cackling of the radio woke Sen from his slumber. When the cigar got too hot, he opened his mouth and let it drop on his lap. It slowly burnt through his trouser and then singed the hair on his under-belly. He woke with a start and threw the butt on the ground.

Although the cigar had only burnt a tiny hole near a fly button, the room was full of the smell of burning cloth. That was a narrow escape, thought Sen. He switched off the transistor and glanced at his watch. It was well after midnight. He blew out the oil lamp and went to the bedroom.

An oil lamp still burned on the table. His wife had fallen

asleep—obviously after having waited for him. She had not changed nor taken off her jewellery. She had put mascara in her eyes. Her tears had washed some of it on to her cheeks and the pillow had a smudge of soot.

Sen changed into his pajamas and slipped into his bed. He stared at his wife's gently heaving bosom and her open mouth. How could he? In any case, he didn't have the slightest desire. He turned the knob on the lamp. The yellow flame turned to a blue fluting on the edge of the wick, spluttered twice, then gave up the struggle and plunged the room into a black solitude.

The bearer came in with the tea-tray and woke him up. "Sahib, it is after nine. Mem Sahib has been up for the last four or five hours. She has had her bath, said her prayer and has been waiting for you to get up to have her *chota hazri.*"

Sen rubbed his eyes. The sun was streaming through the verandah into the room. His wife had made a swiss roll of her bedding and put it away on the top of her steel trunk. "I'll have my tea in the verandah," he replied getting up. He went in the bedroom, splashed cold water on his face and went out.

"Sorry to keep you waiting. I seem to do it all the time. You should really never wait for me." He stretched himself and yawned. "I am always . . . what on earth."

His wife had got up and while his face was still lifted towards the ceiling, bent down to touch his feet. He was her husband, lord and master. He looked down in alarm. She looked up, tears streamed down both her cheeks. "I am unworthy," she said half-questioning and half-stating her fears. And before he could reply, she drew the flap of her sari across her eyes and fled inside.

"What the hell is all this?" muttered Sen and collapsed into an armchair. He knew precisely what she meant. He sat a long while scratching his head with his eyes fixed in a hypnotic stare on the sunlit lawn. He had no desire to go in and make up to his wife.

The bearer came, looked accusingly at the untouched tray of tea and announced that breakfast was on the table. Sen got up reluctantly. She would obviously not have anything to eat unless he cajoled her. And he was damned if he was going to do

it. Again he was wrong. She was at the table. He avoided looking
at her.

"Tea?" he questioned and filled her cup and then his own.
Once again they ate their different foods in their different ways
without saying a word to each other. And as soon as the meal
was over, she went to her betel leaves and he to his pipe. She
retired to her bedroom. He took his transistor and returned to the
verandah to listen in to the morning news.

The arrival of the postman at noon put the idea in his head.
It was only a copy of the office memorandum sanctioning him
leave for a fortnight. He walked in waving the yellow envelope
bearing the legend—"On India Government Service Only."

"I am afraid we have to return at once. It's an urgent letter
from the Minister. He has to answer some questions in Parlia-
ment dealing with our department. I'll get the bearer to help
you pack while I give the car a check up. Bearer, bearer," he
yelled as he walked out.

Half an hour later they were on the road to Delhi; a little
before sunset, Sen drove into his portico. The son and mother
embraced each other and only broke apart when the bride
knelt down to touch her mother-in-law's feet. "God bless you,
my child," said the older woman, touching the girl on the
shoulder, "but what . . . "

Her son pulled out the yellow envelope from his pocket
and waved it triumphantly. "An urgent summons from the
minister. These chaps don't respect anyone's private life. I simply
had to come."

"Of course," replied his mother, wiping off a tear. She
turned to her daughter-in-law. "Your parents will be delighted
to know you are back. Why don't you ring them up?" A few
minutes later Mrs. Sen's parents drove up in a taxi. There were
more tears at the re-union, more explanations about the letter
from the minister. There was also relief. Now that the bride had
spent a night with her husband and consummated the marriage,
she could return to her parental home for a few days.

Sen spent the next morning going round the local bookshops
and coffee houses. The weekend followed. On Sunday morning,
when his mother was at prayer, he rang up the Director at his

home to explain his return and ask for permission to resume work. "My mother has been keeping indifferent health and I did not want to leave her alone for too long." He knew this line of approach would win both sympathy and approval. The Director expressed concern and spoke warmly of a Hindu son's sacred duty towards his widowed mother. "And we must celebrate your wedding and meet your wife . . . as soon as your mother is better."

"Yes, Sir. As soon as she is up to the mark, we will invite you over."

The mother being a 'bit under the weather' and 'not quite up to the mark' became Sen's explanation for cancelling his leave and not having a party. It even silenced Santa Singh who had planned a lot of ribaldry at Sen's expense.

Days went by—and then weeks. Kalyani came over with her mother a couple of times to fetch her things. She came when her husband was in the office and only met her mother-in-law. It was conveyed to Sunny Sen that, under the circumstances, it was for the husband to go and fetch his wife from her home. Sen put off doing so for some time—and then had to go away on a tour of inspection to Southern India. It was a fortnight after his return that his parents-in-law learnt that he was back in town. The relations between the two families became very strained. Nothing was said directly but talk about the Sens being dowry-seekers and Sen's mother being a difficult woman started going round. Then Sunny got a letter from his father-in-law. It was polite but distinctly cold. From the contents it was obvious that it had been drafted and written on the advice of a lawyer with a carbon copy made for use if necessary. It referred to the advertisement in the matrimonial columns and the negotiations preceding the marriage, the money given on betrothal and in the dowry, the wedding and its consummation in the forest rest house on the Ganges. Sen was asked to state his intentions.

For the first time, Sen realized how serious the situation had become. He turned to his mother. A new bond was forged between the mother and son. "It is a matter of great shame," she said firmly. "We must not let this business go too far. You must fetch her. I will go away to my brother at Dehra Dun for a few days."

"No, Ma, I will not have anyone making insinuations against you," he replied, and pleaded, "in any case you must not leave me."

"No one has made any insinuations and I am not leaving you. This will always be my home; where else can I live except with my own flesh and blood. But you must get your wife. Let her take over the running of the house and become its mistress as is her right. Then I will come back and live without worrying my head with servants and cooking and shopping."

Sen flopped back in his chair like one exhausted. His mother came over behind him and took his head between her hands. "Don't let it worry you too much. I will write to my brother to come over to fetch me. He will go to your father-in-law's and bring over your wife. Before we leave, I will show her everything, give her the keys and tell the servants to take orders from her. When you come back from the office you will find everything running smoothly." She kissed her son's hair. "And do be nice to her, she is only a child. You know how much I am looking forward to having a grandson to fondle in my lap!"

Sen found the whole thing very distasteful. He felt angry with himself for allowing things to come to such a pass. And he felt angrier with his wife for humiliating his mother and driving her out of her home. He would have nothing to do with her unless she accepted his mother. He instructed his cook-bearer about the arrangements of the bedrooms. If the new mistress asked any questions, he was to say that those were his master's orders.

On Monday morning, when the bearer brought him his morning tea, he told him not to expect him for lunch and to tell his wife not to wait for him for dinner as he might be working late in the office. He had breakfast with his mother and uncle. He promised to write to his mother every day to tell her how things were going. "You must try and understand her point of view," admonished his mother. "She has been brought up in a different world. But love and patience conquer all."

Sen was the last to leave his office. He drove straight to the

Gymkhana Club. For an hour he sat by the bathing pool, drinking ice-cold lager and watching the bathers. There were European women from the diplomatic corps with their children; there were pretty Punjabi girls in their pony tails and bikinis; there were swarthy young college students showing off their Tarzan-like torsos as they leapt from the diving board. This surely was where he belonged—where the east and the west met in a sort of minestrone soup of human limbs of many pigments, black, brown, pink and white. Why couldn't he have married one of these girls, taught her proper English instead of the Americanised chi-chi which they thought was smart talk.

The bathers went home. Sen got up with a sigh and went to the bar. He was greeted by several old friends. "Hi, Sunny, you old bastard. What's this one hears about you?"

Sunny smiled. "I don't have to proclaim everything I do from the housetops, do I?"

"Like hell you do. You stand drinks all around or we'll de-bag you and throw you out in front of all the women." Three of them advanced towards him.

"Lay off, chaps. Bearer, give these B.Fs. what they want. What's the poison?"

They sat on the high stools and downed their drinks with "Cheers," "Here's mud in your eye" and "Bottoms up."

"Where's your wife?" asked one. "Don't tell me you are going to keep her in the seclusion of the *purdah* like a native!"

"No ruddy fears," answered Sen. "She's gone to her mother's. Would you chaps like another?"

One round followed another till it was time for the bar to close. One of the men invited him home for dinner. Sen accepted without a murmur.

It was almost 1 a.m. when Sen drove back into his house. He was well fortified with Scotch to gloss over any awkwardness. He switched on the light in the hall and saw trunks piled up against the wall. His wife had obviously come back. There was no light in her bedroom. She must have gone to sleep many hours earlier. He switched off the hall light, tip-toed to his bedroom, switched on the table-lamp, went back and bolted the door from the inside. A few minutes later, he was fast asleep.

The bearer's persistent knocking woke him up. His head rocked as he got up to unfasten the bolt. What would the bearer think of the Sahib bolting his door against his wife? He couldn't care less. The throbbing in his head demanded all his attention.

"Shall I take tea for the Mem Sahib?" he asked.

"She does not have bed-tea," replied Sen. "Isn't she up yet?"

"I don't know Sahib; she has also bolted her door from the inside."

Sen felt uneasy. He swallowed a couple of aspirins and gulped down a cup of strong tea. He lay back on his pillow to let the aspirins take effect. His imagination began to run away with him. She couldn't. No, of course not! Must have waited for him till midnight, was scared of being alone and must have bolted the doors and was sleeping late. But he had been nasty to her and she might be over-sensitive. He decided to rid himself of the thought. He got up and knocked at the door. There was no response. He went to the bathroom and then tried her door again. There was no sound from the inside. He went to the window and pressed it with both his hands. The two sides flew apart and crashed against the wall. Even that noise did not waken her. He peered in and caught the gleam of her glasses on her nose.

With a loud cry Sen ran back into the house and called for the bearer. The master and servant put their shoulders to the door and battered against it. The bolt gave way and they burst in the room. The woman on the bed didn't stir. A white fluid trickled from her gaping mouth to the pillow. Her eyes stared fixedly through the thick glasses. Sen put his hand on her forehead. It was the first time he had touched his wife. And she was dead.

On the table beside her bed was an empty tumbler and two envelopes. One bore her mother's name in Bengali; the other was for him. A haunted smile came on his lips as he read the English address:

"To,

Mr. S. Sen, Esq."

Elysium In The Halls Of Hell

Tireless in his red turban
he plays his six-stringed *ramsha*
like a rickety violin.
He's got silver anklets,
and red betel on his teeth.
His stomp on grass is what
the ardent tourists come for.
They also like the crimson
bougainvillaea, snakecharmer
with his burlap bag of cobras,
his tethered mongoose sniffing,
and those umbrella roofs
of terra cotta, over
verandas with marble arches.
And there are costumed women
with bare bellies who pass
and repass the gate, seen through
the mist of fountains, a flash
of local color. Afternoons
the pool is fine for lounging,
nearly, but not quite, nude.
Even birds upon the grass
are a part of paradise. Peacocks
are commonplace, like jewels
in shops along the corridors.
But I could take these tour groups through
that green wall of leafy trees,
just across the road, in fact,
to where a pig strolls from a shack,
could lead them up that alleyway
of sand, could show them what
they would rather fail to see.
It moans and sighs and the human breath
of it at night can even reach
the hotel's latticed windows where once
the harem ladies strolled, peeked out.

Villagers

They do nothing halfway here,
scatter, hide behind reeds
and corners of clay, peek
over dungwalls—or all rush out
coaxing their nannygoats near,
showing their almond-eyed maidens
as if you must choose or take all.
(Veils drop from stunned faces.)
They drag up on charpoys in dust
their sick and their dying, for your
blessing, for sure as hell
you're ordained by one or more god.
The small boys beg you with smirks
to make them immortal
in one fading snapshot. Yellow
and warped on a wall
it may yet bring good luck.
Right now they're not doing so well.
Water is twelve miles away;
women bring it with jugs
on their heads. The blacksmith
pursues his art by the roadside
as if there's a bronze age up ahead.
All he needs is his fire, his boy,
and his tongs. The oxen need shoes.
Dacoits need pistols, to kill
those of low caste, in some other
village. Next time you'll bring
salve for their sores, a surgeon
to cut off a limb that offends.
At doorways the ladies wash hair
and pick one another's head lice
with the grace of houris of paradise.
If you pause and gaze toward them
they'll stand up and dance,
or so their amused eyes seem to promise.
If you ever come back they will rush
out to embrace you, long lost exile
returned to the dust of your streets.

Purdah

In my rooftop study in India,
sitting by the ancient charpoy
a yard high, with lacquered legs
and marble inlay, a bed fit
for a king, I'm surrounded
by portraits of the Rajput
rulers, at least seven
generations of them, each grim
in his turban, letting his sword
touch the carpet. But just one
picture includes a woman—
In all the dozen paintings,
etchings, and old photographs
there is only one woman
and she is presumably
beautiful though I cannot
be sure because she sits
at her husband's side draped
in a veil like a beekeeper's
gauze. It would be funny
if it were not so sad, my not
being able to see her. She wants
to look out, to gaze into my room.
Her small hand touches the veil
of purdah as if to lift
it aside, but the two
faces next to her are stern,
with terrible fierce glares.
Both hold swords and wear
turbans of power, hair coiled
and held for a strike.
They will not let her
come out into this century,
and her beauty if it was beauty
is lost while behind her
magnesium flares against tile
while I presume that her eyes
were brown agate, her skin
the bronze of the women
of roadsides who cup
their gold hands as I pass.

The Caves

The ancient texts will give you
plenty of reasons there is no God
or if there were how he would not
be half inclined to think of you
or to have made the world and you
in the first place. He'd have had
no interest at all in Matter,
having none of his own to slow him
from his perpetual ethereal travels.
Come to think of it, he wouldn't
bother to travel. Those wits
who sat in caves among carvings
had time on their hands,
so they went on to argue
the opposite—how each effect
naturally is caused by something
we have to call God or Krishna
or Brahma or Rama simply because
he seems to have thought
of everything, then some more
like earthquakes, floods, and the savage
disasters man makes up as if by himself.
Moreover, God maybe gave monsters and devils,
and Ravana, the ten-headed warrior.
These assiduous monks before they were done
filled their caves knee-high with pure logic.
And sculptors carved the walls round,
their dust drifting on manuscripts;
they created stone ladies and angels,
believable visions of lovers.
A man can still fall hard for
a lady in stone, archaic and chipped,
with a belly a million times kissed.
Today the silence hums over
the hazed canyon. The river still cuts
deep into bedrock beneath wading lepers.
And above the mouth of each cave
where a monk spun out reasons and doubts,
a swarm of black bees are at work now,

making honey that drops from wax cells.
These bees could trace their births back
to Ashoka, that great Buddhist king
who left roadsigns for reaching Nirvana,
a city of swans and souls without purpose,
with eight noble paths and no more.

Calcutta

RODNEY HALL

Night comes wheeling in along the roadways
choked with smog: dim cluttered.   Still.

The world of man is paved with people.

Lords of creation, masters over destiny,
shrouded on the endless sidewalk slab
lie like the dead, foot to head
with maybe one bare limb stuck out
careless graceful (a child?) and chilled.

Everywhere a dog now howls
drawing the city to his lungs he gives it
back—his piercing dispossession builds
fades and builds its rancid wish
flesh screwed tight with emptiness.

Delhi

R. PARTHASARATHY

1

The ochre air irritates
the tongue. Dust thickens it.
The squalid city groans

under the loo, familiar
as an ordinary afternoon in May.
It's a cemetery of stones

I see everywhere:
Khaljis, Tughluqs, Lodis, Mughals—
they stick to its face

like turds. When Ghazni knocked,
or was it Clive, we paid off
old scores in our backyard.

Eight hundred years of blood-letting
has made eunuchs of us,
once for all unsettled

our minds. Now, atop the Himalaya
unceremoniously grins
an ominous skull, the sun.

2

Time rests his hand
on my shoulder. Old, I look
every illusion in the face.

My fingers are stiff:
I can't write even two lines.
Letters come in from all sides.

I lay them aside. The days
collapse on the pile.
The hands that wrote them

return, at leisure, to knock
at my inexpectant door at Churiwalan.
The present is troubled

to distraction. There is no respite.
I turn a page: the book lies open.
Or, remember drowning myself

in the arms of that slut
Zohra Jan in an effort
to blunt the pain.

'How can anyone,' I ask, 'forsake
Delhi and its lanes?'
The Angrez impudently rub salt

in our wounds. Our pride
bites the dust.
Still pullulate the decrepit ruins.

Now, blood trickles down
the Jumna, while the Emperor
flies indecisive kites.

Or, mourns in verse his discomfiture.
Listen Zauq, after you,
who is left to speak of Delhi?

3

Short of wringing its neck,
I try every trick of phrase
to cosmetize the blank page:

it refuses to improve. Now,
I prefer to brazen speech.
Knock the metaphor out of it.

A Brahminy kite preserves
the afternoon, as I write this.
Near things distract me—

the lickspittle town,
its back street putrid with empire:
Qutub and Purana-Qila,

scrap of paper blown about me
day after day (their distant
tongue rasps my verse)—

throw dust in the eyes. Will
Indraprastha rise again? The Yamuna
has forever covered its spoors.

Life, at forty-five,
is a breath of fresh air.
The children are grown up.

Their eyes hone
my nights: I soften to the touch.
The wife keeps house.

From afar shapes the poems
till they become familiar as prayer.
To be oneself, strike no postures,

on rare occasions stumble upon
the blessing of simplicity—
I couldn't ask for more.

Landscape With Locomotive

SALEEM PEERADINA

For the man under the bridge
Into whose vision two buffalo calves
Flung off the track, plunge from the sky,
The thud is like a jab in the crotch. His job

He knows is to raise a shout. In a joint
Flutter the storks jump as the wave

Of a tremor hits the ribcages of cows grazing.
Leaping out of sight, a shadow

Chases a dog. For the crows who make capital
Out of anything unusual, this is an event
To report. For children, it is an invention better than
Any play. Banging clothes on the stream's floor

The women stitch a rumor in their talk:
Too muffled for the pile of houses
To cock their ears; too distant
For the blue mountain to show any change of color.

The sky exerts its weight in favor of
Not reacting at all. The trees saw it coming
But rushing to the spot was beyond their power.
The green tips the field has pushed up

Were sucking the light with their eyes closed.
The patch of sunflowers as a witness confuses fact
With melodrama. Having been there the longest, the stones
Prefer to hold their tongues knowing this to be

A well-rehearsed accident. The keeper of animals,
The mother of all calves sobs inconsolably:
The hurt has entered her like news
That happens elsewhere but belongs to her.

One chewing a fruit asks another shifting in his seat
What is wrong. In a hand-mirror held delicately
Between the toes, one examines the contents
Of his nose and tells another how it happened.

On a slope a mile away, a figure
With stick and blanket looks up to see people
Swarming round a train on the bridge. In perfect silence
He tells himself a story with two endings.

Haridwar
(The Door to God)

NADAAN

A cry arose from the deeps of dusk,
And moved upward like a wail on trees,
Then sank into an inarticulate whine,
To become its phoenix.

The sorrowing leaves, the anguished birds,
Echoed the stillness that contrasted
With the violence of the assassin,
The blood throbbing with the rhythm of blood.

The bestial cry dissolved itself
Into a vast syllabic pine.
He threw the corpse into the Ganga,
And hid himself in a shrine.

Then arose the chanting of *Hari Om*,
From the killer's heavenly abode,
Mingling with the music of the night,
It rode and rode and rode.

A dreadful sonority, a gong bereaved,
Making the small still voice
Yet smaller,
His conscience locked.

There he slept unmindfully,
In the bosom of his dearest Gods,
While a mother's heart beat at the horizon's end
For the son who was no more.

Translated from the Urdu by K.K. Khullar

Funeral In Chandigarh

AMRITJIT SINGH

In death, she faces specters
of gods she worshipped in life.
Inside the temple
they vie with each other —
son, daughter, nephew, grandson —
to hold her head in their hands
as the camera-man helps them
proclaim love in death
echoing neglect in life.

On the pyre, she looks aghast.
Her protruding tooth resists
ladles of *ghee* and sandal-dust
poured into her mouth
and over stiff and dangling eyebrows.
We watch the tongues of fire
lick the tiny frame
laid in a cradle of wood
craggy, twisted, hard.

In the prayer room nearby
A graybeard on shaky legs
chants holiness in monotone—
his words lost in a shrill uproar
in the latticed window
where two young sparrows
engage in fierce battle
for the nested space.
Such violence in tiny frames, I wonder,
while others of the kind applaud.

The family settle the account.
The boy with donation box
moves among the crowd,
he knows piety has its uses too.
The priest prays for the soul
sinking deep under cinders now.
All interrupt their talk
to say the expected amen.

Two Poems

SHIV K. KUMAR

At The Ghats Of Benares

Between its carrion teeth
the Ganges can hold three live fishes—
fins, bones, and eyes.

A child's lissom body
in a jute bag;
the warm ashes of a young courtesan;
and once I saw a man ferry across
on a sleazy raft to drop
his pet dog and bless
the sharks that carried the prize away.

A priest's chant
tender but peremptory
churns the viscid waters
into submission.

On the western ghat
a glassy-eyed crocodile dips
into the sacrosanct waters
to cleanse its scales—
its belly mirroring
all faces of death.

A Dark Mood

Not tonight—
        not even if you creep foam-footed
        into the bed, offering the salt-
        taste of your flesh.

How can we exchange nudities tonight
        when the shells on the ocean's bed

are wailing for the dead? The corpse
this morning, slumped at the crossroads,
crying after a speeding car, and
the woodpeckers hammering away
at the shadows.

A man should come to his woman whole—
not when the mind, like a perverted
sunflower, turns its face
to darkness only.

Tonight the fires will only feed
the cold; let us fasten our belts,
observe the no smoking sign,
lying spaced between sombre thoughts.

The Wound

MADHAV BORKAR

In the compassion
Of men,
There should be somewhere
Deep down
A lacerating wound
Oozing like the flow of the Ganges
To wash away
The colored stains
Of the Masks
They put on their faces.

Translated from the Konkani by Olivinho Gomes

A British Military Graveyard
In The Himalayas

TONY CONNOR

This wife, "Much loved, much cherished,"
crumbles among long grasses.
She is no more remembered
than the sad young subaltern
who composed her epitaph,
then went on to die elsewhere—
surrounded by grown children,
perhaps.
                She was "nineteen years"—
whether she died of fever
or in childbirth the gravestone
does not say. Certainly she
was well-born: the other ranks
and their women were buried
lower down — with no such view
of distant Tibetan peaks.
Here, daisy and wild iris
sweeten the indignity
of forgotten vows, and words
the weather has scoured away;
tall pines and a grand vista
stand over the broken gate
like an apter reminder
of Imperial conceit,
where everything is broken: —
tombs toppling, vaults cracked open,
urns askew in undergrowth.

I doubt they'd have allowed me
to enter the gate before
Independence, — certainly
not as a corpse. Even now
I'm incongruous among
these dead Public School tyrants
and the extravagantly

phrased eulogies they composed
for one another. I can't
think of them as *my people*;
only "Much loved, much cherished"—
whose name has flaked from the stone —
moves my curiosity
towards unearned affection.
Indeed, the dutiful men
rotting here at attention,
are nobody's people now —
unless Mr. Chatterjee,
(who owns most of the mountain,
so it's said) claims them as his.

Seven Poems
NIRALA

Don't Tie The Skiff

Don't tie the skiff to this landing-place, friend,
The whole village will ask.

Her laughter rose from these river-steps,
Here she knelt in the water and bathed,
How easily the eyes were caught,
And how the feet quivered.
She said much in that laughter,
Leaving much unsaid,
She heard everything, she was gutsy,
And were her ripostes quick.

Love Song

A Brahmin's son,
    And I'm in love

With a Kahar.
She comes at cockcrow
To fetch the household's water,
    I want her.

Koel-black, ah well,
There isn't much to those hips,
She's unwed, that's
What did it, it's a pain all right.

Every morning she comes and gets us out of bed,
No one else follows her game,
She picks up the big pot and goes out,
    My eyes fix her, I bide my time.

The Betrayal

The face yellowed.
The spine curved. The hands joined.
Darkness rose in the eyes.
Centuries passed.
The great sages, saints, and poets arrived;
Each laid down the law.
    Some said that one is three,
    Others that three is three.
    Some felt the pulse, some watched the lotus.
    Some revelled, some kissed the fingers.
    The people said, 'Blessed are we.'
    But the tambourine held out.
    The mridang split into the tabla.
    The vina became the surbahar.
    We now hear the spinet.
    The day breaks.
    The lips of the four cardinals redden.
    Morning's polecats are like night's.
    The Age of Betrayal betrays us.

All Alone

All alone,
Watching my day's twilight
    Approach.

My hair has turned silvery,
My cheeks have lost color,
I can see my pace slacken;
        The fair's over.

I know I've left behind
Cataracts, swift rivers;
I look back and discover
        I've crossed without a raft.

There Was Mist

There was mist along the pond's edge,
There was a cordon of green and blue leaves,
The mango's branch stretched over the water;
Darkness had pitched its tent,
The place was deserted, a procession
Of fireflies went by,
The breeze smelt of the forest,
The coconuts swayed in succession,
The date-palms stood over everything,
The hidden hawk cuckoo sent up its call,
Jackals moved about freely.
Sunrise — and a star glimmered,
Ripples appeared in the pond,
The star shone in the depths.

Ignorance

Those whose heart's thatch
Hasn't caught fire
Haven't searched all the corners
Of their lives, the earth's riches
Lie buried beneath them, their small
Wishes agitate,
The lamp of frenzy
Doesn't burn inside them,
The sun doesn't brighten their sky,
They don't know
What's given in the book of their lives,
Their strings
Are untuned, their music absent.

Soundings
(A fragment)

Soundings of a perplexed heart,
Unquelled voice, today ungloried.

Translated from the Hindi by Arvind Krishna Mehrotra

Three Poems

ARVIND KRISHNA MEHROTRA

The Telegram
for A.J.

The wick sputters and this
Chirp is from the hopper
In my mind. The floor is
Cold. I dip my toes in
It. Someone pushes me
From behind and my whoo—
Pee plunges into the
Swimming pool's boyish water.
He's running towards the
Bottle-green shore, waving
His arms; his ship anchored
In his mind's inlet; his
Cabined keyboard ablaze.

River Stop

Travelling alone
In the northern mountains
I see the river
Rise along the banks,
Pick up a road or two.
Once or twice a year
It steps ashore
And looks back on the cities
It missed.
The boats watch
From high ground.

Star, oar, and fish
Move across the window
Like three forgetful children.

I measure their sleeves
And make them
Little red coats,
I draw magic circles around them
So they don't lose each other,
They disappear between the unlit hills.

The road to the river
Is lined with trees.
Beneath them small groups
of newly-arrived pilgrims
Await transport.

Engraving of a Bison on Stone

The land resists
Because it cannot be
Tempted, or broken
In a chamber. It records,
By carefully shuffling the leaves,
The passage of each storm, rain
And drought. The land yields
In places, deliberately,
Having learnt warfare from the armies
It fed. The land is of one
Piece and hasn't forgotten
Old miracles: the engraving of a bison
On stone, for instance. The land
Turns up like an unexpected
Visitor and gives refuge, it cannot be
Locked, or put away. The land
Cannot sign its name, it cannot die
Because it cannot be buried, it understands
The language, it speaks in dialect.

Two Poems

RAMAKANTA RATH

The Kerosene Lamp

Kerosene, a little smoke, a flame and some insects
fuse together in this metallic tomb.
Inside the belly of discolored tin, a sea of fire
breaks the waves and burns in the black night of fear.

How docile the burning flame, how submissive the savage fire
to the environs of tin—
a good child, a tamed circus tiger—
as though unaware of the dark metal,
unaware of the heat of the lamp!

Those of you who pack a season's leisure under your lids,
who labor to shift your gazes around,
who have combed your lush hair with fragrant blossoms,
have you ever noticed this burning existence of mine?

And could you ever imagine that I burn with fiery violence
in my average *dhoti* and laundered half-sleeved shirt?

Translated from the Oriya by Jayanta Mahapatra

A Poem from
"Four Stolen Glances at Time"

I am no good at discussing space rockets
and moon landings; truly speaking, I am useless
for almost every job. Only I am on the lookout for Madhavi.
Have you by any chance seen Madhavi? My only ability
lies in tracing the whereabouts of Madhavi.
And really, to find Madhavi is not as easy
as it seems. First, I am not quite sure what she looks like,
nor, for that matter, is anyone.
At times she appears bright and distant as a star
in the moon's vicinity,

and at others, her face, distended as a balloon
in the shouts of marchers,
floats past in the afternoon sky;
some days, she appears as a shadow
under a pine tree in the garden at night,
her nakedness defined by thirty heavenly candles.

Secondly, I am not certain that I am looking for her.
At times I drive her away, abuse her.
It is my youth she destroyed; she, poison
of my purest dreams. With her words
that whore enticed me here—to this place
where twilight is still, immortal.
She is that decaying spirit who frightens birds away—
an unending jungle where
the only sound is the slow falling of rain.

Still I keep searching for Madhavi—not
for her firm breasts nor her slender legs;
these things are no more,
and even if they were, they would not matter,
for that eternal lucidity of hers is my despair,
my secret desire that she and I join together,
a happiness possible with her alone;
all the songs I sing for her are truly those
she sings, hoping for my love.

And you too, Sir, have been searching for Madhavi
all these years.
But will she ever sing for you one line of song?
Even though you possess millions,
Madhavi will not be seen with old men.
Your teeth are no longer firm,
and on your head
the slowly growing bald spot shines.

Translated from the Oriya by Jayanta Mahapatra

Pain

PADMA SACHDEV

This head you see
Is a box of pain
A child's rattle
In which pain
Rolls around
Again and again
There are many kinds of pain
The pain of memory
The pain of secrets
Vainly kept
The pain of today
And of tomorrow
But there is one pain
which never throbs,
It just *Is*.
This pain
Is born of
That sorrow
Of which I shall not sing today.

Translated from the Dogri by Iqbal Masud

Dawn

SHAMSHER BAHADUR SINGH

Working the day break
My mind solves the night's blue-black:
    A conchshell deep in tide pool,
    Slate smeared with wet ash;
Catches now the saffron crack:
    Streak of thick, orange chalk,
    A woman's body stirred up
    In a cold spring lake.
With one white stroke,
Sun rises, resolves the sky.

Translated from the Hindi by James Mauch

Three Poems

GIEVE PATEL

I Am No Good

Am willing to concede my uselessness.
To disappear this instant
Seems a logical fate. Should
Nothingness, or a something that
Just as well may be else, assume
Elaborate form: changing with age,
Yet etched into such identifiable
Flesh? If each of my functions could
With ease be performed by
An infinity of men, why preserve
A mock-up of feature and
Frame? Collapse!

Just Strain Your Neck

The tarmac outside my clinic
Flows thick and befogged spirits
Drop in on me, demanding
A simple, eternal whisk to safety.

"A large city," she says, "but to me
It offers no place to sleep."
Woman so impossible that one by one
Father, friend, brother, and husband
Have left her adrift.

She speaks across my tableful of quiet drugs,
But the tablets quiver inside their factory packages.

The sexual odor of rejected women overpowers me.
I am called grotesquely to account
For ecstacies they may have missed.
I am a chameleon about to swallow a nauseous butterfly.
Look, I'm turning green.

To the gods that manage eggs and seeds
I have to say:
The four winds are in your control.
Who and what would you blow
At me with needs
That will not be met? Or why not
Shake us up like impersonal blooms
To charge the wind? Then reaching out
To currents of air would be all
The effort needed, the destitute never
To lose heart in their truant healers;
Just strain your neck, and catch a waft
Of thriftless benedictions.

Public Hospital

How soon I've acquired it all!
It would seem an age of hesitant gestures
Awaited only this sententious month.
Autocratic poise comes natural now:
Voice sharp, glance impatient,
A busy man's look of harried preoccupation—
Not embarrassed to appear so.
My fingers deft to manoeuvre bodies,
Pull down clothing, strip the soul.
Give sorrow ear up to a point,
Then snub it shut.
Separate essential from suspect tales.
Weed out malingerers, accept
With patronage a steady stream
Of the underfed, pack flesh in them,
Then pack them away.

Almost,
I tell myself,
I embrace the people:
Revel in variety of eye, color, cheek, bone;
Unwelcome guest, I may visit bodies,
Touch close, cure, throw overboard

Necessities of distance, plunge,
Splice, violate,

With needle, knife, and tongue,
Wreck all my bonds in them.

At end of day,
From under the flagpole,
Watch the city streaming
By the side of my hands.

Of Garlic and Such

Dilip Chitre

Praise the garlic for its tight
Integration of cloves and its white
Concealment of unbearable astringence.

Praise the onion for keeping
Its eye-opening secret
Under so many identical skins.

Praise woman for her genderless
Passion hidden in a familiar body
The rippling enigma of her inner form.

Then damn yourself
Lord of nothing
Sheathe your murderous sword.

One Touch of Garlic

ASHOKAMITRAN

I opened the refrigerator and the few lingering traces of sleep left me. I knocked on the door that opened into my friend's room. The third time it was not just a knock. The door opened and he stood in the gray flannel shirt I saw him in during all the mornings of our shared residence in the apartment. "What is it?" he asked, his eyes still heavy with rudely interrupted sleep.

"See here," I pointed to the refrigerator.

"What?"

"Garlic."

"What garlic?"

"*Your* garlic."

He put his nose to the open refrigerator shelves and drew back his face. He asked again, "What garlic?"

Nobody could miss the reek that filled every bit of space in the refrigerator.

"What garlic! Everything in the refrigerator is ruined by it!"

"There is no garlic. I didn't put any garlic inside."

"Then who put it? I don't use garlic at all."

"I don't either. There is no garlic smell."

He turned back, went into his room and slammed shut the door.

I felt I had been declared knocked out even before the fight started. How was I going to put up with this man and his garlic for the rest of my stay in Iowa City?

I poured out some milk from my day-old milk carton into the saucepan and boiled it. Added a glass of water and boiled it again. I poured the steaming milk into a large cup and dissolved a spoon of instant coffee and some sugar in it. I took a sip. It was still there, the garlic smell.

Now he also came into the kitchen and placed his skillet on the stove. The stove had four burners and we shared two each. I watched for him to react when he opened the refrigerator but he had the same wry look and took out his bacon block from the freezer. He peeled out a slice and laid it on the skillet. The oblong piece soon shriveled, crackled and oozed out fat. He had almost burnt a side when he turned it over. It made more crackling noises, and he took it out and laid it on a plate. He took slices of bread and toasted them in the bacon-fat still simmering in the hot skillet. Then he sat facing me to eat his breakfast.

I never ate anything that early in the morning. Usually I needed a cup of coffee soon after I woke, but suddenly even that was making me too conscious of an uncertain stomach.

A day later I noticed several people, not as thin as I, pick up a different kind of milk carton at the store. That was low-fat milk. Low-fat milk was my sustenance from then on.

He drank cups and cups of green tea with his bacon. He topped it with a large glass of cold milk. In those days when everything in the United States was a novelty for us and when every moment brought a new discovery, we had talked and laughed over the most trivial of things. His own bacon, for instance. He ate bacon for breakfast because that was the only thing he knew how to cook. Just as I drank coffee because that was the only thing I prepared with some degree of success. Now even that was out. Nobody drank garlic-flavored coffee.

I threw away my coffee in the sink and left my saucepan and cup on the table unwashed. I realized later that I slammed the kitchen door when I went back to my part of the apartment.

*   *   *

Just two days after I had arrived in Iowa City in October of 1973, all the participants of the Writing Program were taken to a place called McGregor for a boatride on the Mississippi. We were more than 20 men and women, and our introduction to one another was a recurring confusion. We did a lot of smiling, asked one another much too often the names and the countries we came from. Peru was mistaken for Chile, Brazil for Argentina, the Republic of China for the People's Republic of China. The Indonesian did a lot of talking though few could understand him. At any given opportunity, some members sprang into a dance or burst into song, not as much to show off as out of a sense of desperation, to be able to communicate *something*. Nobody made a mistake about my country—I was very Indian, with very brown, very dark hair and a hundred pounds to my five feet six inches. But my name was a challenge to West and East alike. After one or two tries, I wrote out my name in capitals for them to read for themselves. That wasn't very successful either—never was a combination of English letters more mystifying. Tymoteusz wasn't difficult. Andrzej wasn't an impossibility. Everyone seemed to know Jacek was pronounced Yatsek. But Thyagarajan was *never* Thyagarajan.

The following week there was again a trip en masse to Des Moines. It was then that he and I became close to each other. He was from one end of Asia and I from another; we were both prose writers. We sat together, ate together and when on an occasion the whole gang had to stay in a motel, we two shared a room. We entertained ourselves by manipulating the air conditioner and playing the multichannel music. We pushed all the keys and buttons but the TV wouldn't work. There must have been some kind of a master switch for the set but we couldn't find it and so returned to music. Country music, classical music, pop music, jazz. There was a bulky volume of the Bible. Gideon's. We read the Bible. Then talked. I agreed with everything he said and he agreed with everything I said.

A few days later the program director had a problem. Another writer from Europe was coming with his wife and there was no accommodation for them in Iowa City. We were already 20 participants, each occupying a whole apartment. If only two could share an apartment. I don't know whether anyone else was asked. But when I was asked, I said, why not? When he was asked, he said, why not? We were spending most of our time together anyway. And I moved into his apartment.

All the Mayflower apartments were designed for two residents. Though they seemed like equal halves, one was more equal than the other. One had three cupboards while the other had only two. Then the pantry. There were four shelves but two were directly above the refrigerator. Only a more-than-tall person could make full use of those shelves. But I didn't really mind. After all, one of us had to put up with the less equal half. And I was the taller of the two.

The refrigerator was a common one. I kept my milk and vegetables and butter in it. I threw that butter out in a few days. Too heavy. Some yogurt and cheese. Fruit juices. He had a number of suspicious-looking things in the freezer and in his half of the refrigerator. Varieties of meat. Eggs. Bottled stuff with strange labels. Maybe they were his native pickles. Or sausages. One he called gravy. Once upon a time the mere sight of meat would turn my stomach. But here I was, sharing a refrigerator, with more than half of it filled with different parts of different animals. But packaged meat didn't smell, at least not as much as garlic did.

* * *

Hunger is a good discipline—Hemingway said that in 1956 of himself in 1926. I returned from the university to my apartment that afternoon and my discipline was very good. I hadn't discovered vegetable pizzas and hadn't known I could get sandwiches with just cheese and vegetables. Pies were too sweet and ice cream too cold. So again and again I struggled over rice. Rice that would be burnt at the bottom. Rice that would be too soft on the surface but hard and uncooked at the core. The right proportions of water and rice continued to elude me. I hadn't known that the stove flame could be adjusted to give the right amount of heat. So I had fruit juice for breakfast, lunch and dinner. Drank coffee at all times of the day and night. And fruit. And biscuits. (Called cookies there.) Today I did my cooking and sat down to eat with the sticky lump of rice and yogurt. The yogurt cup had an airtight lid. So the yogurt was saved, but the cup and the lid smelt of garlic. I emptied all the contents on my plate and placed the cup and lid as far away as possible.

I had eaten my ascetic lunch but still sat on at the table. I was worried. I was unhappy. After all, he too was not used to keeping house and cooking his own food. He was as much a stranger to the United States as I was. I was sure he missed his own people and his own native food as much as I did. If he were to cook his lunch this afternoon, I was sure to see him fry bacon. In a flush of happiness at seeing several meat varieties in the shelves of the supermarket, he had bought a lot of them and stuffed them in the freezer. They must all have been frozen solid by this time. Probably gone bad.

He did come into the kitchen to cook his lunch. "Hullo," I said. He said, "Hullo." He took out his skillet. Then the bacon. Bread.

"Didn't see you at the English-Philosophy Department today," I said.

"I didn't come. I had an overseas call."

"From your family?"

"Yes."

I couldn't imagine my wife putting through even a local call. The nearest telephone to my home in Madras was a hundred yards away, in a shop. I didn't think she would ever think of the telephone to reach me. If she did—got the local exchange and from that to another exchange, from that to another, and from that to the Iowa City exchange and then finally to me—all we would exchange would be hullos. "Hullo, hullo, is that you?" "Yes, hullo, hullo, is that you?"

"You seemed angry in the morning," he said.

"Forget it."

"I haven't kept any garlic with my things."

"But what is in that plastic box?"

"Which one?"

"The one behind all your bottles."

"That? Jae gave it to me. He is the only fellow from my country I know here."

"Couldn't you have kept it closed? It seems like a garlic concentrate."

"There is no garlic in it."

I didn't argue with him further. No use, really.

But after he ate his bacon and toast he went to the refrigerator and took out the plastic container. Now he was a little hesitant.

"Don't you think I am right?" I asked.

He threw the contents of the container violently into the sink. And opened both the hot and cold water taps as well as the mechanism in the sink which cuts up the solids thrown in it. The whole thing made a frightful noise.

"What are you doing?" I asked alarmingly.

"If this is the thing that makes you angry, I will never eat it."

"I didn't want you not to eat it."

But it was all gone down the sink. The whole kitchen was now filled with the smell of garlic. I opened a window and he another. Despite the tension we sat facing each other. We had eaten our sparse lunch, we were in the kitchen, but food was farthest from our minds. I thought I would never again be hungry. Not after what had happened today.

"Did you receive your ticket for the play?" I asked him.

"*Cabaret?*"

"Yes."

"Yes. I got mine. You?"

"I got mine too."

"They have said find your own transport."

"You know where the theater is?"

"No."

"Not far from here. We can easily walk the distance."

We seemed to have exhausted everything under the sun we had to say to each other. The kitchen was getting chilly and I got up and closed the window on my side. He rose and did likewise. Again we sat facing each other in silence.

I didn't want to start the conversation again myself. I didn't want to be the first to break up the meeting either. I waited for him to go to his room. He didn't. After a long while he said, "Some people have too many problems."

"Who doesn't have problems?"

"True, but some people have more problems than other people."

"Come on," I said. "You know all about the story of the woman who went weeping and wailing to the Buddha. 'Show me one human being who hasn't had a bereavement and I will bring your son back to life,' Buddha said, and the woman went away and never came back."

"It is not my son. It is my mother."

"Is she not well?"

"She has been admitted into a hospital."

So that was the overseas call.

"Is it very serious?"

Now he held his head in his hands and said, "I don't know. I don't know."

"Was she all right when you came here?"

"She was in very good health when I left my country. I have never known her to be ill. Now she is in a hospital."

I didn't tell him, don't worry yourself too much, it serves no purpose. He would know it, too.

"Very sorry," I said.

"That is all right."

He rose and went into his room. I got up and went to my room. We both closed our doors very gently this time.

A little while later he came to me. He was dressed to go out. "Sit down," I said.

"No. I've got to see Jae. Will you do me a favor?"

"Sure."

"I am leaving my door unlocked. If there is any call for me, will you take it? Or tell them I will be back at 5:30?"

I didn't say, why don't you tell the telephone people. I said, "I will. I am not going out anywhere this afternoon."

He seemed to have shrunk, to have grown shorter, smaller. He came from a short race but they said that even in those parts, the new generation had larger bones and were growing taller and bigger.

I stayed in my apartment all afternoon though the day outside was beautiful and inviting. I feared I might doze off, so went into the kitchen and made myself another cup of coffee. I felt I was getting used to uncommon, pungent flavors in coffee. Garlic had wonderful medicinal properties. They gave tons of garlic to women in India soon after confinement. Said to loosen up congestion of the chest and several other parts of the body. Improved your digestion. And, of course, anyone would keep a respectable distance from you.

There was no call for him, though I waited tensely for one.

I took a peep into his room. It made me sad suddenly. He had taken out his suitcase and had packed up his things.

He came back earlier than 5:30. And he didn't mind my having opened his room. I shook my head to say there had been no call. He seemed a little relieved. But he could also have become more anxious. No news is *not* good news on such occasions.

Now the telephone rang and both of us sprang toward it. He unhooked the receiver and sat on the floor with it. Yes, it was again an overseas call. He talked fast and then listened grimly for a long while. Then talked. All in a language which seemed to abound in ha's and ah's. I couldn't even make out from the rhythm and cadence of it whether they were communicating happy news or unhappy news. I stood near him all through the conversation which neither side seemed willing to terminate. At last he held out the telephone in my direction and I placed it on the hook.

He sat still like a statue. I asked him, "Who is it from?"

He didn't answer.

"Who talked to you? Anything bad?"

Still he didn't answer.

I called out his name. I said, "Please tell me. You *can* tell me."

Now he spoke. He just said, "My family."

"What is it? How is your mother?"

"She died."

"When?"

"Three hours ago."

There was a vast continent and a wide open ocean between him and his mother's corpse.

I flung myself down and threw my arms around him. I held him very tight almost to the point of suffocating him. He broke down and wept. He wept aloud for several minutes and I did nothing to stop him. My shirt got wetter and wetter around my shoulders. After a long time he grew calm and I released him slowly. He said, "I will not forget you. I will not forget you."

I am sure he hasn't forgotten me. I haven't forgotten him. Nor that evening in his apartment in Iowa City when I held him so close. There was a faint whiff of garlic coming from him.

Four Poems

DILIP CHITRE

Evenings in Iowa City, Iowa

For Danny Weissbort

On top of being a foreigner
I am already an old fart
In this pimple-faced town
Infested with poets and decadent dons
Columbuses on Guggenheims
Magellans on Fulbrights
Vasco da Gamas supported by National Endowments
Set out from this little port to discover
The world we left behind
Statistics show that about the age of forty
Most men go berserk
Even those to whom their women try to be extra kind
Are we already bitter or are we still bewildered
Filling our brown bags with the bounty of America
Wandering through libraries
Boozing and growing long hair or beards
The true exterior of the expatriate
And conversing in exasperated voices
Sometimes even writing poems
While the natives mow their lawns

One Day You Wake Up

One day you wake up and find
The whole country dead.
So what do you do?
Bathe once again in the sacred sewer
And start addressing
Another hymn to the Sun?
And if there is no Sun to such a day,
What do you do?
Perhaps you would already be tired

Of reinventing the dead, even if the temples
Be still standing and the scriptures
Remain unobliterated.
Perhaps you would not find such a day
Extraordinary in the least.
After all, the vedas were not written by man,
And thus your religion has already absolved you
Of responsible guilt. So what do you do?
Would you find that the structures of your mind
Dissolve no sooner than your neighbors disappear?
Or would you be happy to become
A benevolent dictator with no subjects to rule
And therefore, for the first time ever,
A patriot beyond question?
For all that, you might still prefer to be
A traitor among stupid people
Trying hard
Not to die.

I Laugh. I Cry.

I laugh. I cry. I light candles. I drink wine.
My eyes are still dirty with love. My mouth
Fouled by song. Poems grow like lice in my hair.
Said the romantic. Sitting in a speakeasy in Bombay.
The wooden benches blackened by the sweat of years.
The bare bulb casting its poor haze in the room.
Madonna and the Holy Child fading on the wall.
Adding some more soda to the tragedy we gulped it down.
One said Asia was on fire. Another said India would rise.
Outside Bombay lay like vomit. Phosphorescent in the night.
Pardon us our ignorance and our jammed traffic O Lord.
The stale aroma of fucking behind florid curtains.
Forgive us our collective noise and our voicelessness.
From such large visions we fall out into muddy lanes.
We walk narrowly escaping life at one o'clock in the
Morning just when our day ends.

Dhulia

I will retain the British spelling
This dusty town sounds no better in Marathi
We drove in a jeep a hundred miles it seemed
To the foothills of the Satpura
The name of the river is Tapi
The British spelling will not do this time
These tribes are supposed to be indigenous
Though there was a time when all of us were called natives
The women keep their breasts naked
Living beyond the borders of our knowledgeable and dirty eyes
I am beginning to understand what it must have been
For Kipling's kind surprised by such life in the jungles
Even the three-headed god with his shepherd dog
Is a product of an alien technology
Watermelons grow wild where this river unbends itself

Three Poems

DEVDAS CHHOTRAY

Sunday

Innocent girl, once Sunday comes I'll give you
Everything. Marvelous flowers, like eyes,
And a drop of blood pure as a flower: I'll give you
Everything. I'll steal the unmindful, weary sunset
From the Bazaar in my town; from my mother,
The years she has to live; from my little sister,
Her sinless hands (without her knowledge).
Darling, I will fill your belly.

The flowers, the blood, the sun: all these
I'll steal for you, innocent girl, once Sunday comes.
But Sunday will never come. Not until you arrive
Shod in your torn shoes; not until the hard-working god of time
Falls asleep. Sunday
Will never, never come 'til you commit
The world's most innocent sin, beside me,
Naked, in a closed room.

Translated from the Oriya by Jayanta Mahapatra

Fear

What a kingdom you have brought me to!
A cold sun hangs at arm's reach,
a white eyeball. The wind writhes
helplessly like a fish hooked at the end of a line.
The street is festooned
with the naked corpses of boys
for the guest who'll arrive at high noon
in a red limousine.

Here, I lie attired, a white lily
wrapped in a silk scarf, the stars flickering;
your face appears, mournful in anguish;
what a country you have brought me to!

More intricate than the navel,
morning comes, hesitant and afraid,
like a guilty man.

If something shatters today;
if the street floods with a yellow viscous liquid;
if, on this afternoon
a headless man arrives in a red limousine;
And if I quiver in fright,
impaled on a sharp star,
will you take me to your home again,
or hide me like an embryo in your womb?

Translated from the Oriya by Jayanta Mahapatra

Birthday

I feel contented. Flowers have bloomed, filling earth
And sky. Rain has washed away the leftover season,
Washed away the satisfied flowers and fruits.
Friends wipe their own blood away cautiously in front
Of their mirrors. And in both my eyes, and in my tears,
The sinless city appears.

The road shines brightly. Married women
Smear their courtyards with dung. A boy,
Washed and clean, wanders toward the gallows. Inside,
Someone strikes a tin can to the beat of harsh music.
After noon, a chariot enormous as a glistening peak
Comes gliding in from a friendly town.

I feel contented, though my unforgiving face
Hangs everywhere throughout the city; though
A black butterfly hides in my wife's hair, and
My grovelling mother wails in the distant temple.
I am contented even though my dead body lies stranded
In a tunnel like a wounded boat. Broken bones appear,
White, forked. My old blood, turning into a
Bright light, faces me with contempt.

Translated from the Oriya by Jayanta Mahapatra

Salabhanjika

A. D. HOPE

Salabhanjika, inmate of my house,
You have hung for years over the kitchen sink,
Cut from some brochure about Indian art.
My wife, my niece, to fortify their vows
Against the insidious lures of meat and drink
Pinned you, voluptuous, by their diet chart.

My own response to your delightful frame,
Those generous breasts, the bold haunch, the full thighs
And rapt face—did it seem to dream or brood?
—Has naturally been not quite the same:
Symbols of plenty to my masculine eyes,
Abundance and promise, grace and plenitude,

And mystery: India, from which you sprung,
Its arts, its past and its unnumbered gods,
Was at that time to me almost unknown.
I saw you as a woman, enchanting, young,
And did not know by what improbable odds
My kitchen harboured your smile of ageless stone.

I used to think you, in my ignorance,
One of those lovers who endlessly embrace
At Konarak on its Temple of the Sun,
In every erotic posture known to man's
Power to create supple and sensual grace;
At other times I saw you as a lone

Dancer at some maharajah's court.
The nizam, with a connoisseur's cool glance
Followed the fluid ecstasy of the nautch,
Appraising the pearl his boundless wealth had bought,
Ignoring the exquisite artistry of the dance
In contemplation of his coming debauch.

Mere fancies! Now I have visited your land,
Viewed you and your voluptuous sisterhood

And know you for a goddess of the trees.
Yours is no dancer's pose. As the trees stand
True to the zenith and draw up their green blood,
The classic stance of Hindu dryades,

But older than all Hindu gods, as old
As the first worshippers on that continent,
You stand, straight torso, weight upon one foot,
The other drawn back and poising to withhold
Its touch, the arms uplifted, the knee bent . . .
The legend was: one kick against the root

Made the tree blossom from contact with the heel
Of any beautiful woman, but blossom more
Caressed by such a spirit of the wood,
Since all trees have a deep desire to feel
A woman's touch and will give all their store
Of nectar, colour, fragrance if they should.

The legend charms me, I do not think it true;
And yet I long to put it to the test.
Now I am old and, in my season of fruit,
Shrivelled by drought, I too would turn to you,
If by contact with foot or lip or breast
My buds might burst or water drench my root.

Bring me, Salabhanjika, what your smile
Portends, that miracle of late blossoming.
But, till that moment comes which sets all free,
Pause, let me feel my new sap rise awhile;
Then, flood me with that providential spring,
Touch, tend and make me flower, I am that tree.

Three Poems

AMRITA PRITAM

You Do Not Come

Spring is waking and stretching its arms,
Flowers weave their silk threads
For the festival of colors.
You do not come.

Afternoons grow long
Red has touched the grapes
Sickles are kissing the wheat.
You do not come.

Clouds are gathering.
Earth opens its hands to drink
The bounty of the sky.
You do not come.

Trees murmur enchantment,
Airs from the woodland wander
With lips full of honey.
You do not come.

Seasons wear their beauty,
Night sets on its brow
A diadem of moon.
You do not come.

Again the stars tell me
That in my body's house
A candle of beauty still burns.
You do not come.

All the sun's rays vow
That light still wakes
From the death sleep of night.
You do not come.

Translated from the Punjabi by Charles Brasch

The Pariah

Years ago
you and I went our separate ways
without regret.
Only one thing I never quite understood
when you and I said good-bye
and our house was sold.

Some empty vessels lay outside
in the courtyard
staring at us.
Others lay overturned,
hiding their faces.
A wilted creeper
climbed down the door,
complaining perhaps to us
or the water tap
about inadequate water.
All these are now memories long lost.

I only remember
that pariah
who for some unknown reason
entered our empty room.
And the door was locked
from the outside.

Three days later
when the deal was clinched
our house was sold.
We exchanged the keys for money.
The new owner
was shown each room.
And in one room we found
the corpse of that dog.

I have never heard that dog bark.
I only remember the smell of its corpse.
That smell still haunts me.

Translated from the Punjabi by the poet

My Address

Today I effaced my house number
the name of the street at the outset.
I wiped away the direction of every road.
And still if you must search me out
just knock at the door
in each street of each city of each country
it's a curse, a benediction both
and wherever you find a free soul
            —that's my home!

Translated from the Punjabi by the poet

The Image

V. G. BHAT

On the back of this wind,
an image must be carved—
all else is preparation for it,
this flesh, this learning,
birth, death and suffering.
This is no soft wax
and the chisel may blunt—
it must be whetted often
against water and dust.

Time slips through—
the chisel splits
and must be cast away—

another birth may have to be taken,
since the image must be carved.

For whom? Why? Exactly what image?
ask not.
On the back of this wind. . . .

Translated from the Kannada by K. Raghavendra Rao

Inheritance

PRANABKUMAR MUKHOPADHYAY

You were thirty-one when I entered,
Now, at thirty-one, I stand before you today
Face to face, straight;
You, in the oil portrait on the wall,
Seem so complete, content and happy
At sixty-two,
With a faint smile on your lips,
Looking out winklessly day and night.

Your eyes, chin, hair, the twitch of your eyebrow,
Are resemblances of faces familiar
As do the yellowed albums hold
Many a fleeting moment.
Now once more you stand as if in your own world
Thirty-one years back.

I stand before you today, face to face, straight.
Look, I stand so close to you;
Yet a strange gorge opens up in between
And breaking the inheritance throws us afar.
The dome caves in,
Your bright background fades away ever and ever.

Translated from the Bengali by the author

Path
(Padhai)

PUDUMAIPPITHAN

An expanding darkness,
a black enveloping darkness
unknown to man
beyond thought.

Above, a ceiling of darkness,
around me on all four sides

banks of darkness.
The moving feet
devised their own path,
but there is no road
devised as such.

There is rest in death,
but before that
not a moment's rest
for my aching feet.

There isn't the one
to ask me to stay,
while I wander
not knowing where
or why.

I have walked,
I walk
I keep on walking
in the dark.

Translated from the Tamil by P. G. Sundararajan

Six *Jejuri* Poems

*From a sequence of poems about Jejuri,
a temple in Maharashtra*

ARUN KOLATKAR

A Scratch

what is god
and what is stone
the dividing line
if it exists
is very thin
at jejuri
and every other stone
is god or his cousin

there is no crop
other than god
and god is harvested here
around the year
and round the clock
out of the bad earth
and the hard rock

that giant hunk of rock
the size of a bedroom
is khandoba's wife turned to stone
the crack that runs right across
is the scar from his broadsword
he struck her down with
once in a fit of rage

scratch a rock
and a legend springs

The Door

A prophet half brought down
from the cross.
A dangling martyr.

Since one hinge broke
the heavy medieval door
hangs on one hinge alone.

One corner drags in dust on the road.
The other knocks
against the high threshold.

Like a memory that gets only sharper
with the passage of time,
the grain stands out on the wood

as graphic in detail
as a flayed man of muscles who cannot find
his way back to an anatomy book

and is leaning against
any old doorway to sober up
like the local drunk.

Hell with the hinge and damn the jamb.
The door would have walked out
long long ago

if it weren't for
that pair of shorts
left to dry upon its shoulders.

The Horseshoe Shrine

That nick in the rock
is really a kick in the side of the hill.
It's where a hoof
struck

like a thunderbolt
when Khandoba
with the bride sidesaddle behind him on the blue
horse

jumped across the valley
and the three
went on from there like one
spark

fleeing from flint.
To a home that waited
on the other side of the hill like a hay
stack.

An Old Woman

An old woman grabs
hold of your sleeve
and tags along.

She wants a fifty paise coin.
She says she will take you
to the horseshoe shrine.

You've seen it already.
She hobbles along anyway
and tightens her grip on your shirt.

She won't let you go.
You know how old women are.
They stick to you like a burr.

You turn around and face her
with an air of finality.
You want to end the farce.

When you hear her say,
"What else can an old woman do
on hills as wretched as these?"

You look right at the sky.
Clear through the bullet holes
she has for her eyes.

And as you look on,
the cracks that begin around her eyes
spread beyond her skin.

And the hills crack.
And the temples crack.
And the sky falls

With a plateglass clatter
around the shatter-proof crone
who stands alone.

And you are reduced
to so much small change
in her hand.

Manohar

The door was open.
Manohar thought
it was one more temple.

He looked inside
wondering
which god he was going to find.

He quickly turned away
when a wide-eyed calf
looked back at him.

It isn't another temple,
he said,
it's just a cowshed.

Yeshwant Rao

Are you looking for a god?
I know a good one.
His name is Yeshwant Rao
and he's one of the best.
Look him up
when you are in Jejuri next.

Of course he's only a second class god
and his place is just outside the main temple.
Outside even of the outer wall.
As if he belonged
among the tradesmen and the lepers.

I've known gods
prettier faced
or straighter laced.
Gods who soaked you for your gold.
Gods who soak you for your soul.
Gods who make you walk
on a bed of burning coal.
Gods who put a child inside your wife.
Or a knife inside your enemy.
Gods who tell you how to live your life,
double your money
or triple your land holdings.
Gods who can barely suppress a smile
as you crawl a mile for them.
Gods who will see you drown
if you won't buy them a new crown.
And although I'm sure they're all to be praised,
they're either too symmetrical
or too theatrical for my taste.

Yeshwant Rao,
mass of basalt,
bright as any post box,
the shape of protoplasm
or a king-size lava pie
thrown against the wall,

without an arm, a leg
or even a single head.

Yeshwant Rao.
He's the god you've got to meet.
If you're short of a limb,
Yeshwant Rao will lend you a hand
and get you back on your feet.

Yeshwant Rao
does nothing spectacular.
He doesn't promise you the earth
or book your seat on the next rocket to heaven.
But if any bones are broken,
you know he'll mend them.
He'll make you whole in your body
and hope your spirit will look after itself.
He is merely a kind of a bone setter.
The only thing is,
as he himself has no heads, hands and feet,
he happens to understand you a little better.

The Rocks

O. V. VIJAYAN

Mrganga remembered many things: walking over the rocks warm with sunset he saw the temple of the goddess on the hill beyond the valley. And tugging at Father's little finger he asked, "Father, may I go to that temple?"

"Why do you want to go?" asked Father.

Mrganga said nothing but trotted along behind Father. The birds shot overhead like the little silver fish of the river. There was the scent of dung in the dust, and the scent of *tulsi*.

"Mrganga," said Father, "you have not answered me."

Mrganga said guiltily, "I want to see that goddess."

"It is a thing cut out of rock," said Father. "I see no sense in going all that way to see it."

It was difficult to make Father understand. All courage left Mrganga as he thought of Father's face growing sombre forbidding him to go. He felt repudiated. Presently he snuggled against Father again for reassurance. There was something more he wanted to tell Father, but it so overwhelmed him that he could no longer articulate it. It was that as he walked over the rocks at sundown, the goddess on the hill made him think of his dead mother.

He had to cross the valley to get to the temple, but the girl next door could have taken him. So he ventured again, "Father, may I go with Sunanda?"

"There is no need to go with anyone," Father said.

There was nothing more to say, and Father and son walked on in silence. The rocks were gentle and warm, and their feel on the boy's feet grew vibrant. In his noontide strolls, stalking the hillsides, Mrganga would come upon the statues of the serpent gods beside the foot tracks or under the strange trees sacred to the serpents. He would kneel before them, and caressing their granite hoods, ask, "O serpent gods, will you bite me?"

"In you we are well pleased," they would tell him. And they would call him to play in their caverns where the lilies blossomed over the deep water and the blue fish, and where the crypts were full of jewels from the serpents' diadems. There were beds for the child to sleep on, cut in rock and smoothed with the warmth of setting suns.

It was just that Mrganga remembered his childhood. For again, the rocks were warm under his bare feet. Far away the forest stood charred. Beyond the forest the poisons churned in the seas, the clouds changed color and the wind swept on with the myriad voices of the dead. Mrganga scanned the forest with his spy glass. He saw her crouching in the charred tangle. He lay his spear down, and as he did so, the palm of his hand was on the rocks. Their touch grew into him and filled him as it did in his childhood.

"Mrganga," said the rocks, "why did you bear the weapon in your hands? You did not want to partake of our peace."

Mrganga was filled with remorse. He wanted to be the child again, in whom they were well pleased. And he remembered the goddess of the hill. He never saw her, never touched her granite breasts and anointed thighs, and so was his innocence wasted away. He wondered if still the temple stood on the hilltop and if the sun set over the hill. No, the radiation must have worn the temple and the hill to dust. Goddess, mother, said Mrganga, why didn't I come to you with Sunanda? While Father slept or was out hunting the little beasts, I could have slipped away.

Mrganga stirred himself out of his remembering. Now the deep experience of the rocks was gone. He broke a charred twig and tied a strip of white cloth to it to make the flag of peace. He walked down towards the forest.

The forest was a giant carcass of gesturing cinders. He stood on its edge and raised his white flag.

"I have come without my spear," he called out. "Can you see my white flag?"

He had to wait a while for the thin voice which replied, "Wait there. I am coming."

She came out of the forest. Mrganga exclaimed in spite of himself, "How terrible! You're burnt all over."

She smiled.

"Why do you grieve over me?" she asked. "Am I not your enemy?"

He caught himself reasoning. He was reasoning like Father would have. This woman is my enemy, he reasoned.

"These are not burns," she said laughing, "but ash and soot I smeared on myself."

She dusted herself clean. Now her skin showed the pallor of the yellow people. She stood before him in her tiny undergarment which sagged below her navel.

"Where are your clothes?" he asked.

"I have lost them all in battle," she said. "No one shall spin and weave anymore."

He moved closer to her.

"Tan Wan," he said. "Can I call you Sunanda?"

"Why?" she said. "Tan Wan is a beautiful name. Do you know what it means in our language?"

"I do not want to know what anything means in your language," he said. "The fathers of my people would have been disappointed in me if I knew."

"Mrganga," she said, gazing with satisfaction at the colors playing on the clouds, "those fathers of the peoples are all dead."

She stood there and with a sweep of her hand turned his gaze to the far horizon. All the way to the burning rim lay the pollen of death, soft and golden like the dust on moths' wings.

"It is just you and me now," she said. "All that is left of the two great armies. We are the last surviving enemies."

Tan Wan pulled off her undergarment. She stood yellow and naked.

"Look at me," she said.

"You are beautiful," he said.

She gazed down her breasts at her own body. She gazed down below her navel.

"Can you see me bleed here?" she asked.

"Yes, I see the blood," he said.

"It is my womb crying," she said.

The cry of the womb went out over the wilderness of the pollen. Mrganga could not hear it, but stood beside her contemplating the far sweep of the dust.

"It is into this pollen," said Tan Wan, "that my son disintegrated. Your spear killed him, Mrganga. And as the thing flamed up his limbs, my little Chen cried, 'Mother, I am in pain'."

She stood a while in that memory.

"Mother, I am in pain," she said. "Sorrow goes no deeper than these few words. Dying, he stretched his hand towards me. He was afraid and wanted to hold mine. I did not touch him. I was a soldier and my duty forbade me. I could not let my hands catch fire. My Chen, who never went out anywhere without clutching my little finger, went, alone."

"If you had caught fire," he said, suddenly triumphant, "and I stayed alive, your country would have lost the war."

"True," she said. "But the nations are dead. And no one walks the earth anymore save you and me. So the computers tell us. Just the two of us."

He peeled the rag off from around his waist. Like her, he too stood naked. Naked, they held hands. Then hands round each other's naked waists, they walked over the rocks. All around them lay the primordial nothingness. The sunset darkened over the dust of plants and insects and machines and fortresses.

"Tan Wan," Mrganga said abruptly, "my daughter was three years old. She would half wake in the middle of the night and if she found me at the other end of the bed, she would roll over to me, and reassuring herself, go off to sleep again. She would smile in her sleep knowing, as one knows in sleep, that I was near. Her name was Sita. Once a girl asked her if her name was Gita. Tears came to Sita's eyes, her lips twitched. She cried the whole day: that girl had called her Gita! I scooped up Sita and smothered her on my bosom and laughed. But as the fire spread over her limbs, again I saw her lips twitch."

A scalding wind blew over the pollen of the dead children.
The pollen rose. The pollen fell and was quiet again. Tan Wan
caressed him below the navel.

"No!" he said. Yet he let her hand be.

"Are you not my enemy?" he said.

"The sun is setting," she said.

Under the darkening sky the pools of lava gleamed. The
pollen gleamed.

"I remember how the dark used to scare him," she said. "He
would cling to me in the dark. Yet I did not touch him."

She turned her face away.

"Tan Wan!" Mrganga said. "Are you crying?"

He was holding her in his arms. She laid her wet cheek
on his shoulder. She pressed her wet lips on his bosom.

"I like your breasts," he said.

Her sobbing ceased.

"They are small," she said apologetically.

He let them spill into his palms and felt their heaviness. He
wiped the lingering soot from them.

"I have seen your women and the goddesses in your temples,"
she said. "I wish I had their large round breasts."

"Oh," he said, "what if you had them?"

She said shyly, "I might have pleased you better."

They walked on over the rocks.

"The cry of my womb envelops me now," she said.

"Mythili," he called her.

"Oh, my lover," she said, "may I kneel before you?"

Tan Wan kneeled. Mrganga towered over her, sorrowing
like a king, looking down on the fullness of her behind as she
kneeled.

The machines that survived over the earth clattered to one
another, communicating passionlessly. An occasional space craft
strayed back home, bearing the body of its navigator.

Tan Wan and Mrganga came upon a patch of soft grass.

"It is not radioactive here," she said.

"The grass is growing," he said.

"Look," she said. "Flowers in the grass!"

They lay down on the flowers.

"Look at the stars, Mrganga," she said. "So many of them, like the seeds of men wasted in the dark. And just as futile. They spin out through the emptiness, fleeing from the emptiness within. So does the child, as he seeks love, relentlessly feed on the moldering ancestor. Bloody murder goes on inside his innocence, molecule chasing molecule, metabolism which knows no mercy. There is injustice and desolation within every created thing."

"Do not remind me," he said.

The grass rose around them like incense and roused them. He caressed her all over. He kissed her thighs and her breasts and the slight slits that were her eyes. He kissed her beneath the navel and on the sacrificial blood.

They woke. Their joy had left their limbs weary. Tan Wan rose and started to walk down towards the forest.

"Tan Wan," he said, "where are you going?"

"I am going to get my spear," she said.

"Why," he said, "It is not day yet."

She did not reply, but walked on. He made no attempt to stop her. Presently she was back with her spear. She lay the spear on the grass and sat down beside him. She caressed his limp organ with gratitude.

"Mrganga," she said, "Your seeds are within me. If you so desire, I will wait for them to sprout again and people this garden. They will become multitudes, great nations. What is your desire, my love?"

"Burn down the garden," he said.

Tan Wan's face shone. She lit the grass and flowers with her spear.

"God of the Vanity of Creation," she said, "we will no more be your accomplices!"

"Love me, my beloved," he said.

She lay on him again for the last act of love. When it was over she wept disconsolately and long.

"My love, my love," she said, "the wars are ending within us."

In infinite compassion she raised her spear and touched him where her tears had fallen. Then she laid it in his hand. Gently he touched her breast with it. The fires began swirling through their flesh.

"Peace, my love."

"Farewell."

When it was over, all that remained was the fine dust of gold.

A wind blew over the rocks, and the rocks awoke to an ancient memory. The memory of salt waves lashing on them, the memory of incipient life. They remembered it unfolding through the ages in death and slaughter. Those ages were a mere instant in Time. The instant had passed. The wrong had been undone.

The rocks had waited for this knowledge. Once again they were lost in their slumber.

Translated from the original Malayalam by the author

Two Poems

I. K. SHARMA

Three Stones

I met three stones of a native rock
on the way: big, middling, small,
a boulder, a road-block, a pebble.

The first was
huge, high, a do-nothing,
resting at a place
simply by the logic of girth and time;

next,
tepid, tardy, uneven,
its bottom smeared with sludge
Janus-like, crying, decrying both;

last,
small, slim, full of grit,
war brewing in its grains
yield not to size, shape, or status
nor to theory of time.

Khajuraho

Here are no sermons in stone.
The figures act: mate and mate
in eighty-four ways and will do so
beyond 1984.
All commandments die here.

My Village Girl

MOHAN SINGH

A bundle of grass on her head
She came, her hips swinging
Like wine pitchers
She, the girl from my village
Pataki and mustard flowers
Like blue and yellow eyes
Peep through the green grass
Long blades of grass
Hang over her eyes
A net of green dreams
Her face caught in it

She lifts her skirt up to her knees
And holds my arm to cross the Suhan river
Ankle-deep water rises to her knees, to her waist,
Her legs disappear beneath the shimmering water,
And her skirt goes up like an upturned umbrella

The water goes down her thighs, her knees, her ankles
So does her skirt
"Thank you, brother," she says
Like a koel cooing from a mango grove
And leaves my arm and goes away
On the sand hill her foot-prints
Gleam like a prisoner's chain
She goes up the mound
Tall and slim like a sugar-cane
And becomes a part of the green tree.

She did not look at me
I could not see her face caught in the green net
But I cannot shake off
The dust of her touch.

Translated from the Punjabi by Balwant Gargi

A Photographer

B. R. LAXMAN RAO

I go to take pictures of a wedding
for money, for pleasure.
The place is full of people-hustle, splendor and gaiety,
the rustling of sarees, the beating of drums,
food, coffee, hospitality. . . .
None invites me to eats and coffee.
I sit in an empty chair in a corner and watch:
the dry chatter of the old, bent with age;
the chirping vanity of over-ripe maidens;
the anxiety of men.

The kashiyatra, dhare, mangalya-dharana etc.—
by the time the various ceremonies are over
I get to know
the lotus-faces of a number of female-jewels—
their glances, laughter, dramatics
and their names.

My side whiskers, goggles, silk shirt
tight pants, pointed shoes
and Tony Curtis smile excite
the curiosity and admiration of a number of girls
and the dumb jealousy of a number of boys.

When I lift my head,
my camera eye sees
a girl, leaning against the stairs,
absorbed, lifting her leg—
and up it goes
till the naked, white flesh of her thighs
and stops
thrilled somewhat.

When they call me for food,
for politeness' sake
I say, "No thank you."

In the evening
in the hustle of the reception,
in the bustle of the music concert,
they gather round me,
shower their affection,
burn with desire,
show off, smile sweetly
smiles of acquaintance,
lift an eyebrow, throw a side glance
and make me feel
my life's fulfilled—
these women, these beauties.

I click the flash at every edge and every curve
and suck in their beauty
into my camera.
At night, before sleeping
I recall their faces one by one
and ruminate:
Radha — Padma — Pankaja — Mala — Vishala —
          Suneeta —
I invite the dreams
in vain, in vain!

At last
the next evening
I hand them over
their respective photographs;
they run their eyes with mutual admiration,
with a catch in the throat they laugh
and go away to their respective places,
leaving behind with me
the fading memories
the negatives
only.

Translated from the Kannada by S. K. Desai

Three Poems

SHREELA RAY

For H.: Three Poems

1

Leaning

against your sleep —
white body
white
daemon —
I forgive you

In this castle—your arms
I who am an arsenal
against myself—
in this moment
in this sleep
in this ceasefire

a garden is possible even
on Akbar Road
and I know the name of the ship
that will take us there.

2

In the times we are together
I have no self
of memory
of you,
color and texture,
time or music,
not even poetry.

Let me look at you
in the half-light
and turn slowly, slowly
to the left

and wait
and turn a little more
and wait again.

When I look at you
I feel rich and lazy:
giver of rice and love.

3

You know
I have loved before this
many times,
and once
specially

and still you keep me,
keep me
in rice and loving.
And there is nowhere I can go
without your mark,
these rivers,
roots and trees
on my groin.

From the Colonies

Father among the dead
who watches over me . . .

The rain does not stop singing
all night in my sleep.

A cloud passes over my hometown.
When it seemed I awoke
there was a mound of ashes at my heels.

I washed my hands in the still
warm dust.

Through all my travels
the smell has stayed with me.

But I have grown uncertain
of whether indeed I heard rain,
or the footsteps of interrogators.

I have decided to say nothing
of what I have seen or touched
because even my spare life
is dear to me.

Dusky Sally

As a young girl
in the evenings, no one came to me
but in dreams—from across the river,
out of a photograph or the pages
of a novel.

He leaned against the pillar
and engaged me in passionate conversations.
I was always ready
in a crisp new cotton sari every day.
I was prepared—
to lose him in an accident or a war
or to a previous betrothal,
or we would grow apart, naturally.

Anyway, I had my pride left,
and that was something.

The Gipsy Girl

U. R. ANANTHAMURTHY

A bunch of burning champaks red
in her hair tied together in a curved knot;
a fish hidden in her thighs; serpents erect
on her arms; in she, the smell, came—
from the backyard where she had stood.

Dark teeth; torn saree; but
laughter, laughter, laughter in her eyes
as if packed tight with light.

With a sacred mark on my forehead,
besmeared with gandha, dressed in sanctity
on the threshold I stood.
Long ago. It was evening then.

Leaning against the tree, she said, "Sir, get
tattooed—it won't hurt; let me do it."
There was mischief in her laughter,
her laughter—
harsh and stern.

I stole my mother's saree, gave it to her.
She stopped.
I stole my father's money, gave it to her.
She stopped.
She laughed—harsh and stern, her eyes
reducing me to a mean, paltry thing.

As if the seed shot roots, and double-born, like a
          Brahmin, split in two,
to clutch the soil ploughed by a Shudra—
laughter, laughter, laughter in her eyes,
as if it was darkness falling. . . .

Translated from the Kannada by S. K. Desai

Blue Eyes

P. RAMA MOORTHY

With you on my bike
I crashed into a car
but we both escaped
what should have been
a total smash-up
or shambled remains.
An hour later
as we sat in deck chairs
drinking tea
you mentioned casually
it was your birthday.
Slowly a thin tear
played on my eye
and I saw how
climbing once
on hands and feet
the unknown side
of the mountain
I had come upon
the mouth of a gorge
where under tangles of vines
a rill pushed through rocks,
poured over a sandy floor
making an oasis.
The spell had got me
and I slid into the pool
scooping out as I lay
precious handfuls
of the first grains of the earth.
But what took my breath away
was a soundless explosion
of a thousand butterflies
sifting the sieved light
of the noon sun
and in that beatitude
I had remembered
what I now see
in depths before me
your blue eyes.

Love Knows No Logic

PANDAV NAYAK

Love knows no logic
Stonewalls do not make a prison
Love and logic lunch regularly
at my table, together
among a crowded haul of wrecks
in the home of my mind.

They eat and leave
nibbling away at my spongy existence.
I suffer your pains
but compose myself again
when we part ways
after eating into each other's pokered face.

They share my bed
and
weave labyrinths over my head
till I know that
my mother's form
and
those breasts of my sustenance
have run into your veins
and cloven into my balls
for a metamorphosis.

In ecstasy
I shoot up sparks
which jerk into
the fluffy cotton of the sky
and settle down.
Does the sky
ever realize them
burning into embers
inside its intestines?

Love and logic even exchange
their pants and shirts

as they stand guard
over my house in disarray.
They cover between themselves
an exegesis
which is fluttering wildly today
(or the mawkish silence grinning?)
against the winds of change
inside a slough
of blind allegiance.

At night
back home
these twin sentinels of humanity
close themselves
against the neon-world
and spur it on
to endless debates and confusions.

Love and logic are
coeval
coterminous
but do not
coexist
like the sky, ocean, wind
and, if you permit
US.

A Poem

DHOOMIL

She knows how many men
have been ripped stark naked
from mere words;
and now people are indifferent towards
killings . . . a mere routine.

She was born of a
vagabond's boredom but
she has eloped to the city
with a literate person.

Even before puberty,
copulating . . . she realized:
love is
a search for an apartment
in a human swarm
even while getting drenched
in an unabated downpour.

She learnt
every girl becomes an inn
accessible to all wayfarers
after the third abortion;
a poem
after the third reading.

No it's useless to look for meaning
in the secret codes of prostituted
language in
the bullock-pissing postulates
all useless.

But if possible, you may tell the man passing by
"Here is your face, mister
you lost it midst the processionists!"

It is enough for the time being.

Long back there was time when—
somewhere in the wilderness even
a man's animality gave out a shriek and
the entire habitation quaked.

But now she knows
a poem is a brief monologue
of a man confounded, beset
and gone berserk.

Translated from the Hindi by Ajit Khullar

Very Close It Was

ASHIS SANYAL

Very close it was you came
            before you turned back,
so there is strong loving rain
            over the wild wide earth
and the horizon still is set in
            infinity because
full-skirted *Radha*, clothed in heaven's gold,
            is as ardent as ever. I
remember walking a long way looking for
            you in early darkness,
one morning and today I still walk, softly
            to wondrous assignations.
In your embrace death and birth mingle.

Yet I do not remember when
            you first came and took
possession of all that I had. In
            what secret spot, where,
did you first disrobe, shapely milkmaid
            delightful as a cooling drink?
Forgotten are the words you said when
            we were alone together.
Alluring, in eternal loveliness, you stand
            between life and non-life,
an unblemished goddess.

Very close it was you came
            before you turned back,
taking with you all I possessed.
            To me you give the ringing earth,
musical from time immemorial and
            the moon's shining touch
immense on the open upland.

      No darkness wearies me any more.
      No grief distracts me any more.
      Unhesitating, in the cold, endangered,

I climb the lightless stairs, knowing it is
    love I want, light I want
and agreeably pleasant company.

Translated from the Bengali by Lila Ray

I Do Not Know
(Theriyavillai)

NA PICHAMURTI

I see the mountain
as rock and stone!
to carve a statue,
to build a temple,
        a compound wall round a bungalow,
to metal the road,
a peak to conquer . . . .
All this I see,
but not the mountain as mountain.

I see the flower:
bait for tender love,
to distil a perfume,
arrange in a vase . . . .
All this I see,
but not the flower as flower.

I see myself:
as a stone pillar
supporting an unseen society,
as the icy pinnacle
of all evolution,
as the last link
in the chain of generations . . . .
All this I see,
but not myself as myself.

Translated from the Tamil by P. G. Sundararajan

Three Poems

KAMALA DAS

The Sea Shore

On some evenings I drive past the cremation ground
And seem to hear the crunch of bones in those vulgar
Mouths of fire, or at times I see the smoke, in strands
Slowly stretch and rise, like serpents, satiated,
Slow, content and, the only face I remember
Then is yours, my darling, and the only words, your
Oft-repeated plea, give me time, more time and I
Shall learn to love. How often I wish, while you rest
In my arms that I could give you time, that this great,
All enveloping thing I offer you, calling
It meekly, love, can take us to worlds where life is
Evergreen, and you, just at those moments raise your
Red eyes at me and smile, perhaps at the folly
Of my thoughts. Shall I forgive the days, that speeding,
Shed as footmarks, the wrinkles beneath your eyes, or
Forgive the crowds who come to you to talk, to plead,
To argue, and the gay brittle ones who flash such
Fake smiles at you and ask you for drinks or are asked
For drinks . . . all those destroying ones who leave you by
Night, to lie so ravaged, so spent, like a sea shore
In empty hours under moon . . . ? Not knowing what
Else to do, I kiss your eyes, dear one, your lips, like
Petals drying at the edges, the burnt cheeks and
The dry grass of your hair, and in stillness, I sense
The tug of time, I see you go away from me
And feel the loss of love I never once received.

The Dance of the Eunuchs

It was hot, so hot, before the eunuchs came
To dance, wide skirts going round and round, cymbals
Richly clashing, and anklets jingling, jingling
Jingling . . . . Beneath the fiery gulmohur, with
Long braids flying, dark eyes flashing, they danced and

They danced, oh, they danced till they bled . . . . There were green
Tattoos on their cheeks, jasmines in their hair, some
Were dark and some were almost fair. Their voices
Were harsh, their songs melancholy; they sang of
Lovers dying and of children left unborn . . . .
Some beat their drums; others beat their sorry breasts
And wailed, and writhed in vacant ecstacy. They
Were thin in limbs and dry; like half-burnt logs from
Funeral pyres, a drought and a rottenness
Were in each of them. Even the crows were so
Silent on trees, and the children wide-eyed, still;
All were watching these poor creatures' convulsions
The sky crackled then, thunder came, and lightning
And rain, a meagre rain that smelt of dust in
Attics and the urine of lizards and mice. . . .

The Testing of the Sirens

The night, dark-cloaked like a procuress, brought
Him to me, willing, light as a shadow,
Speaking words of love
In some tender language I do not know . . .

With the crows came the morning, and my limbs
Warm from love, were once again so lonely.

At my door step I saw a pock-marked face
A friendly smile and
A rolleiflex. We will go for a drive,
He said. Or, go to see the lakes. I have
Washed my face with soap and water, brushed
My hair a dozen
Times, draped myself in six yards of printed
Voile. Ah . . . does it still show, my night of love?

You look pale, he said. Not pale, not really
Pale. It's the lipstick's
Anemia. Out in the street, we heard
The sirens go, and I paused in talk to
Weave their wail with the sound of his mirthless

Laughter. He said,
They are testing the sirens today. I am
Happy. He really was lavish with words.
I'm happy, just being with you. But you . . .
You love another,
I know, he said, perhaps a handsome man,
A young and handsome man. Not young,
Not handsome, I thought, just a filthy snob.
It's a one-sided love,
I said. What can I do for you? I smiled.
A smile is such a detached thing, I wear
It like a flower. Near the lake, a pregnant
Girl bared her dusky
Breasts and washed them sullenly. On the old
Cannon-stand, crows bickered over a piece
Of lizard-meat and the white sun was there
And everywhere . . .

I want your photo, lying down, he said,
Against those rusty nineteen-thirty-four guns,
Will you ? Sure. Just arrange my limbs and tell
Me when to smile. I
Shut my eyes, but inside eye-lids, there was
No more night, no more love, or peace, only
The white, white sun burning, burning burning . . .

Ah, why does love come to me like pain
Again and again and again?

If Return You Must

VASANT BAPAT

If return you must better go quickly
Don't hurt my heart like a lingering sweet night

When you come here again
please forget that wrist-watch, that cage of minutes

Forget your smart cosmetics
Forget your city morality, ironed and tip-top

Forget those flowers in the hair-do
Forget delicate silken frills, forget the tinkling bangles

Forget, friend, the language of movement
Forget those tenses denoting time,
    the adjectives like quick and hasty

Come like the serene ocean-wave
Quivering hiding expectant innerself
    Calmly slow-intoxicated.

Translated from the Marathi by Prabhakar Machwe

She and I

SAMIR PUNIT SINGH (Age 12)

The sky was shining
When we both met.
The moon was up
When we both met.
The world was jealous
When we both met.
But we smiled
When we met.

The love days
Were liked only by us.
The world felt jealous
Even of hearing about us.
The dim bathroom light
Shone brightly when we met.
But both of us were unaware
Of the cruel wide world.

Our last meeting was seen
Only by the bathroom light.
We went our different ways then.
She was taken by the cruel world
And I by loneliness.
Oh, the cruel world.

A Whirl

MRIGANKA ROY

Love was my god then:
My scriptures, my creation, existence and ruin, the cycle inviolate.
In the interlude of elemental nature
I was then a water-bearing stratum of earth, shadow, snake,
            river, tree.

I was then god,
You the goddess, a jolly tree in sky and air;
And I, its thick green bark.

I loved you then:
At dawn like your shadow I fell from your body,
I used to gaze at you throughout the day
Whirling round and round and round the sun.

Your voice was then like milk lately drawn, warm and pure,
Your eyes like the bud of Karavi;
Your breasts like the warm dune,
Torso flowing upwards from the altar of the hips like a fountain,
Sharp and taut.

I loved you then, Karavi:
But who knew in your hungry pistil
Lay the hollow for a poison seed:
A whirl.

Translated from the Bengali by Satyabrata Mukherjee

Loss

BIBHU PADHI

Do I know the words
that would sparkle and shine
in the darkness of grief?
Do I know how to frame the gestures
that would serve
a father's lean body well?

He hasn't lost anything
that I could call mine.
And yet, why do his eyes
look that way, as though
they would strike me blind,
dry up my tears?
Why are they so lonely and hard?

Do I remember his little boy?
Do I remember how
his laugh — loud, without pause —
echoed against the flying birds,
or played sadly inside his house?
Did I take something home
from his laughter,
from the light of his simple eyes?

And because those eyes had something
that I had lost among words
on one sad Indian afternoon long ago,
I have lost him now.

A Hieroglyph of Lost Intents

AJIT KHULLAR

time transformed
my song into
an empty chair
a vacant carrel
an old newspaper
of yesterday
folded thrice on itself
an abandoned chip
of stone etched
with a hieroglyph
of lost intents

Two Poems

DEBA P. PATNAIK

My Father's God

They carried him out that day, threw him
to vultures,
as if
he was dead.

For days and nights
the birds gnawed into his
entrails.

He cried —
ominous, primeval.

Every evening,
my father returns home
like a cowherd boy.

His untimely aged, asthmatic wife
waits for him
with cooked rice,
vegetables, curd.

An old habit,
although
they have been dead for years.

Have you brought the calf
home?
She asks.

No.
Thrown to vultures.
He replies.

For Karunya

We lie side by side. Winter
night howls away. Karunya
wiggles like a lobster, nudges me;
snuggles up, his right leg on my hip;
right arm   stretched across my neck.

Dada   daddy   dada
candy   candy
blum   blum   drr   drr
mama   moon
Nay (Renee)   car   nanni (for banana)
moon   candy
dada

He chants his own lullaby
in a dark room.

Abrupt as lightning, he
falls asleep —
strands of his dark hair
clutched between his lips.

Half-asleep I dream of my dead
mother,
of my childhood
lost somewhere years ago.

Kanya Kumari

LAKSHMI KANNAN

She lived within every woman
this virgin,
reserved, aloof as she
lived even within the twice-married woman
or the one who had given herself away,
Kanya Kumari, the eternal virgin
frozen in history, waiting with pride
for her man, untouched.
Every woman saw herself
frozen for a moment
in that exquisite sculpture,
her pure profile sharply etched
against a flaming sky,
diamond of the purest water
on her nose,
flashing signals to straying ships.

Untouched,
her face looked over and beyond the
waters of the three oceans,
turbulent waves, their fury
matching hers,
Kanya Kumari.

Loona
(A dramatic poem)

SHIV KUMAR BATALVI

Every moment
The fiery serpent
Stings the night
And races down
My spirit's dark desert.
The tortured illusion casts shadows and dances.
I am Loona

Youthful wife of the old king
Weaving a basket of desires.
I sit in my courtyard
The spinning wheel of a long day before me
And spin out the sun's rays
At night I twine the rays into a thick rope
And hang it from the ceiling of my dark existence
This rope of seven strands—
Seven colors of a rainbow—
Is a hangman's noose
Daily it tightens around my neck
And I die every night
I was born under an unlucky star
Oh gods of heaven
I am a living death.

Ira (her friend) replies

Every young woman of this land
Is Loona
And every husband ugly
Every woman's body is a water jug half empty
Every courtyard is cursed by an impotent man
Here every father dreams of incest
And desires his daughter
Every mother dreams of her son in her bed
The stale blood robs the young bride
Every young woman commits a delayed suicide.
Shivering in the lap of her frozen dreams
Burning in the heat of her fiery limbs
Daily twining the rope of sunlit desires
She hangs herself by its noose
She neither lives
Nor dies.

Translated from the Punjabi by Balwant Gargi

In Front Of the Visa Office

BIRENDRA CHATTOPADHYAY

They parted from each other
The two persons
In two paths;
Yet they were standing
So long as they could keep their eyes
On each other's face.

Adieu!
Thus whispered one.
The other felt within
A pain
That of a lost brother.

The two faces
As if of hard stone
Chiselled;
The two pairs of eyes
Lifeless and turbid;
Remembered the same dead father
In equal right;
With terrible brawl in their blood,
Invisible.

And now
If in these days
That face again appears
In remembrance
A bitter failure of sightlessness
Tolls in blood.

Then where
In which path
Shall the two lost brothers stand,
Since the whole sky is covered
By a wall
From top to toe?

Translated from the Bengali by Ramendra Narayan Nag

Going Abroad

RAJI NARASIMHAN

The bed was vast and sprawling with downy satin mattress to rest the body. But the way Nair lay stretched stiff on it, it could have been a bare board. His wife sat at the dressing table in the corner, her back to him. Through half-closed eyes Nair viewed the back of his wife, wishing for nothing more than that she should remain thus forever with her back to him, leaving him to himself. But she turned almost immediately, smiling, and Nair saw the big white teeth between sensuous, curving lips: the big, collyrium-rimmed eyes like a cow's: the round, coin-like cheeks like a doll's. With a soft moan, Nair closed his eyes fully, all he could do to shield himself from her stark presence.

"In these foreign countries . . . they wear gowns, is it not?" Her dragging voice thick with her unsullied Malayalee accent assaulted his ear.

Nair shut his eyes closer, stiffening against her giggly irreverence about a subject like going abroad. Slabs of color and darkness danced inside his closed eyes. He jerked them open again, his poise almost completely gone.

His wife sat smiling broadly at him, not wanting an answer to her question, only the pleasure of asking it. Of course they wore gowns abroad, didn't she know it, her smile said.

"When we go abroad shall I also wear gowns?" Laughing, she inclined her head coquettishly.

Nair gazed at her with listless eyes, thinking, his luck was probably already ravaged with all these reckless conversings of hers. At this very moment, possibly, Mr. Barnes, the English gentleman on the board of interviewers who had interviewed him and others for teaching positions in Brunei, was composing a letter of appointment to him, saying, "Come without delay. We have much pleasure in announcing your appointment." But some counter-force from his wife's rantings had probably already travelled up and intercepted the decision taking shape in the Englishman's mind. Telepathic communication was not unknown!

Nair did not have a very clear idea of the kind of place Brunei was. But it was advanced, he was sure. Didn't the presence of an Englishman on the interview board prove that?

"Shall I also wear gowns?" his wife asked again, mirth thickening her voice.

Nair swallowed his temper, turned on his side to look with dull stupor through the balcony at the scene outside. The entire length of the littered pavement below was creeping with beggars. The whole day long they squatted there, swaddled in their rags. Stiff, matted locks like cacti came down their necks and they had a quivering, scurrying vitality to them like roaches or sewer rats. When he tore his eyes away from the beggars and looked into the distance he saw a landscape of scabbed housetops. Beyond that were the swaying tops of palm trees, forever doing their slow, incantational dance against the tropical sky of the township.

A hand nudged his shoulder. His wife's steamy breath fluttered above him and she pressed her face to him, leaning over him in one of her spells of amorousness.

"All the time . . . " she murmured huskily into his ear, joining her gaze to his in looking through the balcony at the swarming pavement below. "All the time they are there . . . these wretched vermin. Dirty . . . dirty . . . "

Nair shifted on the bed without making his irritation too obvious. She glided in beside him just as though he had made way for her eagerly. Digging her chin into his shoulder, hands loosely over him, she rocked them both together, humming a baby rhythm. He closed his eyes to forget the crush of her body.

"See, see," she tautened above him suddenly. "Somebody. See."

A woman had got out of a rickshaw. A young woman of a type not seen in these parts. A spring to her step, a buoyancy not known in the liverish township. A young man was with her. He looked like her husband. But it was the personality of the young woman that was raising all the stir on the pavement.

She stood there on the pavement, a brilliant figure in her purple sari. Stepping sideways in a light, impulsive movement, she said something to the rickshaw puller while handing him his fare, that sent him away laughing. Looks from bystanders were being thrown at her, at the travelling suitcase in her hand, and at the man with her: bold, forward looks because she seemed to invoke boldness, forwardness.

Nair turned away abruptly, seized by a sudden premonition that he was condemned to spend all his life with his prattling wife.

"A woman ought to be . . . smart." He tried to sound impersonal, but the reference to the sprightly newcomer standing there on the road was too obvious.

Apprehension rose in his wife's eyes. "Yes. Yes. I also think so." She turned ingratiating, supplicating. "Yes." Pushing her fingers through his hair she twirled it round and round, attempting kiss curls.

He jerked away. She felt like crying. What was he thinking about, what was there on his mind? Silently, she cursed the slick, laughing outsider who brought with her disharmony, unsettlement.

Nair presented himself at the bungalow one week later. Facts about the pair had circulated in the meantime. They were passing through. They were both lovers of antique objects. They were both fascinated by the heavy, carved door frames of the township, remnants of European colonization. He rarely noticed these doorways himself. They were too much like the township. Footfalls sounded in the hall and the girl stood before him.

His mind blurred. She was risen from the wind, he thought, in a wild burst of fancy. Her eyes arched back towards her temples like twin steeds bracing under the reins.

"Hallo!" she sang.

"Hallo!" he responded instantly.

"Hallo-o!" she sang again. "Do you know, I expected you to come? Well, not you precisely, I suppose. Not you as an *individual*, I suppose, with your precise turn of nose. But you *generally*, you know . . . as a sort of UGR . . . "

"UGR?"

"Unofficial General Representative!"

Laughter, both his and hers, merged and cascaded down. In the momentum of it he stepped over the threshold of the bungalow.

"O, but it's a darling, this town. Exactly like a little town!" she sang on.

"There are too many beggars. I loathe them." He turned gruff at the thought of the beggars.

"O, but I would overlook them, you know. I would just turn a blind eye to them, you know. There's no place in India free of beggars, is there?"

He paused, thrilled. It seemed a pregnant, wonderfully illuminating remark to make. "Yes. Yes. I see your point. Yes. Everywhere there are beggars," he repeated her remark joyous. Corridors far back in his mind opened, the suffocating beggar presence of the town seemed less suffocating. Wasn't it so everywhere?

She tripped along ahead of him into the house, turning round to look back and smile encouragingly at him, inviting him to accompany her in.

"It's a marvellous house, isn't it?" She turned back once more, her voice ringing out in the vast, empty hall.

He thought it was just a crumbling old tomb, in tune with the derelict state of the town. But he was ready to see the house with her eyes, see magic in it if she said so.

"The walls are quite strong, actually." He ran his finger-tips over the peeling plaster of the wall, hummed a fraction of a tune, stepped out lightly into the back garden. She wasn't going to let that old nuisance, Critical Sense, spoil her pleasure in communicating with the small town mind. "Beautiful, don't you think?" She waved her hand over the expanse of the garden.

Again, Nair was puzzled. The garden was little else except a wilderness of bush and creepers. Some palm trees pushed up through the tangled growth, their crested tops waving against the sky. He didn't care for palm trees from such close quarters.

"How little is needed for human happiness," her voice throbbed.

He was moved. "It's a lovely breeze," he said enthusiastically.

"Coffee?" she nodded up at him with dramatic eagerness.

"O, yes! Wonderful!" It was all some marvellous pattern of living that she was revealing to him, he sensed, standing facing her in the wild back garden of the derelict bungalow. He was suddenly curious about the crockery she was going to serve the coffee in. They would be marvellous, of course.

"You have nice cups?" he asked gaily.

"The thickest of clay pots! Black!"

"Black! Black cups!" he was astounded.

She smiled delightedly. "Dug them from the bottom shelf of the Handicrafts Board. Bullied dopey salesgirl into going on her knees to get them, practically!"

"Really?" How amusing, making a girl crawl like a baby!

The palm trees swayed languidly in the corners of the back garden. Quickly Nair drained his coffee, shifted his chair a fraction of an inch, rested his head on the back of it. The palms met his eyes and beyond the palms was spread the ultramarine sky of the town.

"I want to go away."

"Abroad?"

"Yes!" He sat up. He'd known she would understand. "There's no *scope* here! Fellows not even matriculates are earning four-figure salaries!" Reddish brown flecks appeared in his eyes. "I am an M.A. first class. Honors graduate!"

"You will not be respected in a foreign country," she reasoned with him. "Colored people are not, you know."

He resented being called colored. He didn't however, mention Brunei. He wanted to hear her out first.

She sat up straight, carried away by persuasive fervor. "It looks glamorous from a distance, you know. But it's totally misleading, believe me. You're put on the fringes of society there . . . "

He looked attentive, but far from convinced. "You have been abroad?"

"Well," she faltered a fraction, recovered quickly, making a small gesture of dismissal, her voice trailing off. "Well, I have . . . "

"For higher studies?" His voice was hushed with respect. "Went on a scholarship or something?"

"Well, actually, it was an Art course." Her voice trailed off again.

"You are an artist." Nair was overwhelmed.

"Well, actually . . . " she laughed, made the throw-away gesture of dismissal again. "Just drop pebbles one by one into the Hudson River, lady. You'll get nice patterns that way." Her Art Instructor's voice rang in her ears. She stilled it. There were things far greater in life than Art, she was discovering every day. But of course conveying any idea like that to this man of essentially limited understanding was out of the question.

"Where? New York?" Nair's heart raced wildly at the very mention of the place.

"Well, yes, New York." For the third time she made the throwaway gesture.

"New York." Nair looked at her with veneration. All her earlier remarks about colored people and favoritism vanished from his mind. She was an artist, she had had experience of foreign countries. "I shall also go," he said, his throat aching with longing.

He shifted his chair to ease his racing heart. And then, eyes glowing, he began telling her about Mr. Barnes, the English-man on the interview board, the letter he was going to get from him any day now.

She was a good listener. She had cultivated the art of listening.

The melancholy figure of his wife stood at the balcony of their house when he came out.

"You went to a strange woman's house," his wife sobbed. All strange women were improper, sirens from strange lands, sorceresses.

She wasn't a stranger. She was that only in the barest technical sense, he wanted to snap at her.

Face lifted in pose of high tragedy that came so easily to

her, his wife sobbed at him for cruelty, negligence of her own feelings, of herself.

Again, he caught himself from snapping at her. The beggars were out there, swarming over the pavement. The obscene, rat-like energy they exuded beat down any stamina he might have had for argumentation with her.

"Let us go to get our photographs taken for our passports, shall we?" In something of a stupor, an oppressiveness in his chest, Nair moved over to his wife, patted her on the hand. "Let us get our photographs. And also our vaccination certifi-cates. All our documents must be ready, don't you think? Who knows when the orders will come? Any minute they can come. There are a hundred and one things to be done, you know. Let us make a move."

"Photograph? I must change my sari?" Her tears stopped and she clung to his arm. "And for the vaccination — they will poke the needle here, like this, is it not?" Raising her forearm, she jabbed her finger into her own flesh, laughing up at him.

Whiffs of her strong body odor rose up to his nostrils, and he stood suffering her weight and smell, just as he always had.

She changed her sari, and they came down to the road. Nair looked across at the bungalow. He tensed. The woman was standing at the front door. His whole being braced in a swift desire to dash over to her, stand by her side and thus re-state their get-together of a little while ago. But his desire braked — almost the instant it dawned. There was a man standing with her. That was her husband, he realized, returned from his antique-collecting. She was laughing at something her husband had said or something she herself had said to him. Nair couldn't determine which. Heart bounding, he watched them. She was laughing with her husband exactly as she had with himself in the afternoon earlier, syllable for syllable, it seemed to him. An eerie feeling gripped Nair. He felt that with every syllable of laughter, every toss of head accompanying the laugh she was wiping away some portion of himself, his own image imprinted at that doorway where he had stood in the afternoon, and was substituting that of another man. He wanted to cry out, do something decisive to arrest this extinction of himself that he was witnessing.

"Come on, come along," his wife tugged at his hand. She had put on a nylon printed sari of large tulips, her face bleached with talcum.

He braced again to break away from her but it was too public, he realized and restrained himself. Just behind him was the row of beggars importuning all and sundry with equal, overpowering energy. And behind the beggars stood the woman at her front door, laughing in repetitive fervor that made him feel worthless, depersonalized.

His wife tugged at his arm again. Stepping dodderingly as though over sand, Nair moved down the road with his wife in search of a rickshaw that would take them both to town for their photographs.

The Secunderabad Club

J. BIRJE-PATIL

The Empire rests there.
Dull cherry orchard thud
Of cues from the Billiard Room,
Heirloom of a half-finished game.

Bearers in white man this khaki outpost,
Playing host to snickety ghosts,
Mutton-chop good looks, peaches and cream,
Flash on their sepia consciousness.

Someone dissolves with a cool splash
In the desegregated pool.
An irate Koi-Hai glares,
Thumps the table with a pseudo-Sandhurst air.

On the wainscot of the Men's Bar,
Mid-century Club Presidents turn brown:
Their portraits shine in the mirror—
None breaks rank.

To whom do these memories belong?
They sprout in vases,
White ants building colonies,
Chota pegs served for auld lang syne.

Out in the dark a cart creaks by
In the land of the vanishing empires
Adipose waddlers chew betel-nut
In the corridors of power.

Bearers stoop under the white man's burden.
The Empire is frozen
In their look of reproof
As fish-knives are used for stirring the soup.

Three Poems

JAMES NOLAN

After the French

In the manicured square
the frogs are gargling
and the beggars turning
over on the sidewalk
in their rags. O
another night of it!

Pale women in shiny saris
slide by in closed rickshaws
with tiny yellow flowers
woven through their hair.
They are speaking French.

What is there to do
in a French colony
after the French have left?
Watch the lizard on the wall
above the light bulb waiting

for an insect, fall into the lazy
overhead mantra of the fan,
contemplate the cloud of mosquito
netting suspended above the bed,
close & open the screens & shutters,

rock all day in your underwear,
occasionally snap to attention,
salute the air and swear.
There is nothing, nothing
to do in a French colony
after the French

but to remember, try to forget
a world as far away
as the Faubourg Saint-Honoré.

This evening, as I droop
with heat like a banana leaf

over the balcony railing,
an Indian boy, a creole boy,
zigzags below on a bicycle
and calls up
bonsoir, monsieur.

The Pilgrim & The Monkey

*Who sees variety and
not unity wanders from
death to death.*
—*Katha Upanishad*

1

Is this the way to see India?
To disappear into a locust cloud
of lunghis shoving onto a bus,
arriving at Cape Comorin,
where the three seas meet,
months later, on the wrong train,
smelling of sandalwood paste?

There the pilgrim sees
that even these crows pecking
at the cracked asphalt street
are waterbirds on the back
of a 5000 year old elephant
wading in the grasses of the Ganges.

2

Or, consider the spider monkey
scampering over the temple gopuram:
it moves up & down, across & back
over the swollen towers
swarming with stone gods
& goddesses, garishly painted.

O the many armed
& elephant-headed,
the lizard-tailed
& swivel-faced,
all the possibilities of human
& animal forms entwined,

and this monkey, nervous, distracted,
wiry as intelligence, almost human,
scurries from one to another
gone mad as the mind turning over
& over the original oriental puzzle.

Tiger Watch

*Periyar Tiger Preserve,
Kerala, India*

"Americans," the guide
explains to the villagers,
pointing at the moon.

Here the immense green
breathes as one unbroken
skin: we are specimens

and this the opposite of a zoo.
We live behind barred windows,
surrounded by a 10 ft. tiger pit,

while waves of harmony build
and subdue in the soupy heat
as if conducted by invisible hands:

wild boar, leopards, barking deer,
elephants, gaurs, mongeese,
myna, barbets, babblers, bulbuls

and tigers. Every evening we mount
the steps of a rickety watchtower,
lightmeters set at infinity,

to watch for one. They never come.
Chain-smoking in asthmatic torchlight
we are observed by the cat-eyed night

bristling, loose-jointed, long-tongued,
which wraps us up to smell us
then throws us back. As mystics

for angels we wait for them
but only the moon appears,
porthole through which we fall

like vinyl waxdolls into a world
we can kill but never see or own.

Moonlight Poem

BIBEK JENA

Here, once, was moonlight.

Once, someone stopped crying
And some of us
Carried the corpse of that cry
On our shoulders, through acres of moonlight.
The corpse burnt, afterwards,
We discovered (under the dense banyan tree in the dark)
The wind lying helpless, hands and feet bound,
Its mouth gagged.

Was it possible for us to return, together, from there?
And if we did return, each one alone, to some corner
Of his own,
And there sat through our own muffled crying,
Knowing no one would take notice, would we grow quiet?
Would it be for that wind which lay bound hand and foot?
Or, for that cry which had been burnt to ash?
Or, for the lush moonlight that once was there?

Here, however, there was once moonlight.

Translated from the Oriya by Jayanta Mahapatra

To Golconda, with William Meredith

S. KRISHNAN

*The Golconda Fort, outside Hyderabad, with
granite walls covering an entire hillside, served
its rulers as stronghold, administrative capital
and marketplace. Tané Shah was the ruler who
kept the sainted Ramdas imprisoned in the
Fort for several years.*

You simply must climb
    Golconda
They said to William Meredith

Watch girls
Buy pearls
Go to a mushaira
Or do something
But you simply must . . .

So we climbed Golconda
Three hundred steps
One for each of Tané Shah's
    wives

As we huffed our way up
We paid silent tribute to
    Tané Shah
Who called on his ladies
    nightly
Though always in a palanquin

The rock spawned the fort
And the fort spawned Tané
    Shah
Those are not roots on the
    stony rubbish
They are Tané Shah's palan-
    quin-bearers
Who have called it a day
To palanquin-bearing

Tané Shah sat upon his throne
dispensing justice from a
        height
I shot an arrow into the air
meaning it for Tané Shah
But the cunning geometrical
walls around him
Made it ricochet and
plunge into my chest

Bad fellers coming so Tané
        Shah had birdgirds the
        guide said
It took a little worrying and
bodyguards emerged
Epicene laughter filled the
        chambers
from the faces of Tané Shah's
        eunuchs
Guarding his three hundred
        ladies—
and the guide smirked

The Persian wheel turned over
and over again
Greased by the marrow of a
thousand slaves
And sent water up the hill
to Tané Shah's palace

Up on the hill Tané Shah
washed his limbs
While his palanquin-
bearers spat blood
Getting ready to take him down
and bring him back up
There were many of them

William Meredith shrugged
and said
The stones are arranged nicely.

Two Poems

AYYAPPA PANIKER

Beograd

When I see the washing
hung up to dry
behind open windows, how do I
feel reassured of man
and his vision.

Some hands
turned rough with the wringing of clothes
have fashioned with love and tears
those folds
that now compete for warmth.

The wind blows
and the windows close
but through the chinks
tiny eyes smile at light.

Here is light, warmth, love

Here is life.

Moskva

All lands look the same from the air
Only he that looks deep down sees the difference
The colors and shapes that spell the character.

In Mayakovski Square
Under the shadow of the muscular masculine figure of the poet
A woman sat munching brown bread and spitting into her hands
The satchel on her lap full of odds and ends
Babushka Russia was chewing the tobacco of history
Her spittle lent color to her wrinkled palms.

Swan Lake was on in the Tchaikovski Hall
Gossamer notes merged into diaphanous dreams
But the booming cars on Gorki Street muffled the voice of pain.

The poet leaned forward to touch her forehead
He stroked her tousled hair famished and grey
Like the bare skyline of the city around.

Two Poems

ASHOK DAS

Cuttack

Here
the winds are words
and words are winds.
And those
who travel beyond
them
are dead stones
beside an unending street
of no return.

Graveyard

Forgotten
hearts sleep here
eating
silence
      sod
      by
      sod.

Calcutta

RUTH FAINLIGHT

Carts loaded with sacks and planks
moving into the pre-dawn city.
One man in front between the shafts,
two pushing from the back.

Knees drawn up to the chin,
rickshaw-men asleep
on the poles of their vehicles—
black crows roosting.

A five a.m. sweeper,
stiff-legged, stooping
at an empty crossing
by the silent kiosks.

The gaunt fronts of hospitals,
their windows bright
as strings of colored lights cascading
down this wedding pavilion.

And now the airport bus goes past
another drug-store, another clinic,
the Panacea Laboratory,
another sweet-shop.

Dark brick obelisks and pyramids
along the ruined paths—
". . . guide on young men,
the bark that's freighted with your country's doom":

Derozio's memorial—
and Rose Aylmer dead
in the Park Street cemetery.
Blood and marigolds at the Kaligat.

Give that girl thirty pice
because she's singing.

But don't look at the lepers'
blunted fingers.

In the Tibetan Restaurant, drinking gin,
middle-class intellectuals
to whom the greatest insult
is to be accused of pity.

Midnight

KEDARNATH SINGH

Just at this hour
the night starts peeling off her dark clothes
and in the street are heard
the footfalls of the street's last man returning home.

Just at this hour
all of a sudden
all the street-dogs start barking in unison
and on the river gets printed
the truest and most dreaded poem of my time.

Just at this hour
rings a bell
and under a certain law of this town
patients on hospital-beds
and actors on the stage
    give up the ghost.

Translated from the Hindi by G. Asthana & R. K. Sharma

At Crossroads

S. S. MISHA

Dark is the night —
Lamps all off
Only a dim and deadly night
Of the crossroad pole stands,
Not a streak of light elsewhere.
Stung by the snake of darkness
The city sleeps like the dead.
Sighing in deep remorse
The wind is losing breath.
The dark and deadly tongues of darkness
Have poisoned the breath of the city.
How bad, how sad and helpless.

Cold is the night
Hardly a heart with streak of light
Feelings going cold and numb
Consciousness getting deaf to dumb
Difficult to know what to do
Dark and chilly all directions
How to leave the crossroad light

Lead moulding into the bones
A dark cover has wrapped the truth
Senses do not work at all

Dim and deadly light of the crossroads
Cannot show the path to be trod.
At best it sighs in sympathy
And stammers to tell the truth.

Let darkness be the watch and ward,
The city is not without inhabitants.
Why not muster courage and heart
To knock some door and try a luck.
Little be the hope — if not even that
Why not make an effort at least.

Translated from the Punjabi by Gulzar Singh Sandhu

The Fish

VINDA

There's a fish on the sitar of Ravi Shankar,
much like a fish, yet more than a fish.
His Om-shaped eye, swollen with tears,
staring from below
through the waters above
at the firmament of stars;
swimming in the deeps
profound with fragrance
and densely shadowed with champak trees;
flowing through the golden tumult of the flood
into the ultimate poise of the major beat
yet more than a major beat.
There's a fish venturing in the restless rhythm,
abstracteyed, crosslimbed, incarnating,
exploring the rocks, battering the shore,
heart-shattering like anguish;
yet more than anguish.
There's a fish like the memory of the crescent moon
in the mind of the darkest night.
Its glide is much like Urvashi's brow,
yet more than that brow,
abducting the reckless senses to an exotic realm;
a glide, responsive to rhythm;
a glide, ecstatic in its nudeness;
a glide like the border of the sari teasing the female breasts;
yet more than a border.
There's a fish swimming in the bass,
yet more than that bass;
oceanic in extension,
approximating the Onkar,
closing the alternatives,
the usurper of a deluge,
infinitely infinite, yet more than that infinite.
There's a fish on the sitar of Ravi Shankar,
much like a fish, yet more than a fish;
his Om-shaped eye, swollen with tears.

Translated from the Marathi by the author

Two Poems

EUNICE DE SOUZA

Idyll

When Goa was Goa
my grandfather says
the bandits came
over the mountain
to our village
only to splash
in the cool springs
and visit our Lady's Chapel.
Old ladies were safe
among their bags
of rice and chillies,
unperturbed
when souls restless in purgatory
stoned roofs
to ask for prayers.
Even the snakes bit
only to break the monotony.

Mrs. Hermione Gonsalvez

Mrs. Hermione Gonsalvez says:
In the good old days
I had looks and color
now I've got only color
but just look at my parents
how they married me to a dark man
on my own I wouldn't even have
looked at him. Once we were going
somewhere for a holiday and I went on
ahead my hubby was to come later
and there were lots of fair
Maharastrian ladies there and they
all said Mrs. Gonsalvez how fair and

beautiful you are your husband must be
so good-looking too but when Gonsalvez came
they all screamed
and ran inside their houses
thinking the devil had come.

My House is Afire

BALAKRISHNA SHARMA

My God, my house is afire, it is ablaze.
Someone breathes in my ear, O senseless, awake, awake.
I am indolently lying down, stretching my legs.
Shutting my eyes to the huge loss I will take.
All that is mine being consumed while I wait for aid.
Even now this my mind will not shake
off. Someone breathes in my ear. Awake, awake.

The fire of desire, the fire of wrath is ablaze
Here the fire of rancor, there of hate.
The volcano is smoking, the ground has been shaken away.
My foes throw colors of flame from the bonfires they make
In my house. My house is afire, ablaze.

Should I say that these fire-makers are foes or friends?
Without their presence, human meaning ends.
They make me shudder in their fiery ways.
My white swan's mind blackens, chars to a crow's.
O my house is afire, it is ablaze, ablaze.

Translated from the Hindi by Josephine Miles

Towards Delhi

KUNWAR NARAYAN

Whoever the horsemen are leading,
I have seen being dragged
many times before.

Hands tied, in captivity once again,
Who was he? I cannot say,
For only two tied hands
Reached Delhi.

Translated from the Hindi by Vishnu Khare

The Release

SHIV K. KUMAR

It was the quietest day of the week—comparatively speaking, of course. Only one death reported in the press— 'of a member of the minority community' shot by 'some unknown person,' from a speeding jeep, near Red Fort. Although censorship had sternly warned all media against identifying any community or individual so as not to incite communal passions, it was never difficult to guess which community had committed aggression in a particular incident. For instance, from the report of the solitary killing that morning, it was clear that some helpless Muslim had been gunned down by a fanatic Hindu as yet another act of vendetta for what Hindus were alleged to have suffered in Pakistan. But now it appeared as though Delhi had run its course of arson, rape and massacre, and was gradually settling down to an even pace of life.

Many European and American observers believed that by suddenly withdrawing from the Indian subcontinent, in that scalding August of 1947, the British had astutely exposed the utter incapacity of the 'natives' for self-rule. No wonder, the free Republic of India had voluntarily chosen to install a member of the British royalty as its first Governor General. Lord Louis Mountbatten was even nicknamed Pandit Mountbatten as though he were Jawaharlal's first cousin! As a counterthrust, a section of the Indian press played up the whispering scandal about Lady Edwina Mountbatten and Pandit Jawaharlal. So the least India's first Prime Minister could do for his paramour was to maneuver her husband into India's first Governor General-

ship. But neither Mountbatten nor Nehru could calm the frayed
tempers of the Hindu refugees from Pakistan who were now
lusting for Muslim blood.

In the early afternoon of that quiet day, a young man, in
a light grey tropical suit, got out of a taxi at the mouth of a
narrow street, and began to jostle his way through a crowd of
shoppers who were picking up their groceries before another
spell of curfew would immobilize life in the capital.

There wasn't much rush farther down the street where a
few Tibetan pavement vendors had spread their wares — coarse
woollens (sweaters, stoles, scarves, stockings, gloves), necklaces and bracelets in colored stones and beads, and tiny gods
and goddesses in bronze. Behind a low wooden table, used as a
bargain counter, a young vendor's wife was feeding her little
baby — her moist nipples partly showing through the slits of
her *choli*, while her husband held up a bronze idol of Lord
Shiva to a lanky, indifferent customer whose eyes had meandered
toward the young mother's ripe breasts.

The man in the grey suit also glanced at the Tibetan woman's
partially exposed breasts, but he didn't stop. Anxiety rippled
all over his face. After emerging at the other end of the street,
he turned sharply round a corner and strode towards a cathedral.

At the main gate, he paused for a few minutes, flicked a
speck of dust off his jacket, then trudged towards the bishop's
residence across a vast courtyard. But even before his hand
could reach out for the bell, the door opened, as though auto-
matically, and an English priest in a crisp white robe peered
out.

"Mr. Gautam Mehta?" he said, raising his right hand as
though in benediction.

"Yes, Father."

"Come in."

Gautam Mehta took in the bishop at a quick glance. He was
a medium-statured, stocky man in his late fifties — a sallow
face, sea blue eyes, a bulbous nose, a sagging jaw and high cheek
bones. The hair on his head was sparse; in fact, a round patch
of baldness was showing just above his forehead. But what held
Gautam's immediate attention was a pair of hands — white, soft

and sensitive — hands that must have been moulded by years of prayerful posture in making offerings of love, compassion and forgiveness.

The bishop led his visitor through the drawing room to his study, a small oval-shaped room stacked with books. On the front wall hung a large canvas of wounded Christ in the lap of Virgin Mary, which showed Jesus's face, petulant and confused, like that of a soccer center-forward knocked off his feet near the goal. Gautam wondered if the painting had been done by some casual pavement artist — a work of haste and indifference. In a corner stood a small aquarium with some Chinese goldfish frisking about in limpid water.

Pointing to a padded leather chair, the bishop said:

"Won't you sit down?"

"Thank you."

"It's much quieter here . . . I guess the city is calm today."

"Yes, Father."

"I hope it stays so."

"I hope so too."

"But one never knows."

"No, Father."

A white cat with black whiskers slunk into the room, stared sharply at the visitor, then glided sinuously towards the bishop who took it up gently into his lap and began to caress its nape. His mobile fingers now ran up and down its fluffy back. It purred, then closed its eyes as though in serene composure.

"A very pretty cat," Gautam said, more as an ingratiating gesture than out of any appreciation of the animal's beauty.

"Yes, indeed. Belinda is just adorable."

A brief pause.

"Would you care for a soft drink, Mr. Mehta—a lemonade or a pineapple?"

"Please don't bother."

"Do have something. It's a scorching day."

"A lemonade then, please."

Carrying Belinda under his arm, the bishop disappeared into the house and Gautam heard him ask someone for two lemonades. But it was a gracious voice as though he were asking a favor. Gautam now somehow felt assured of his mission, though his face still looked tense.

A cold sensation ran down his spine. No, he mustn't give himself away, he told himself. He must marshal his memory to quote promptly and aptly from the Bible to pull off the entire operation. For the past one month, he had given the book the same close study as a medical student would give to Gray's *Anatomy*.

Still holding the cat under his arm, Father Jones returned to his chair. He was followed by a dark man with two lemonades on a china tray.

"Thank you," Gautam said to the servant, taking one glass from the tray.

The bishop also said, "Thank you, Samuel," as he put down Belinda to take the other glass.

The servant withdrew immediately. The bishop then swung in his swivel chair to pull out an envelope from the top drawer of his rosewood desk. Holding it in his right hand, he said:

"But I must confess your letter hardly said anything. I got nothing out of it."

"I'm sorry. I was perhaps too confused and nervous."

"Maybe if you had telephoned me, we could have at least talked before . . . "

If the bishop's tone had not been genial, Gautam would have sensed something irascible about his words.

"Writing, I guess, comes more naturally to me than speaking."

"Indeed, I should have thought so," Father Jones said, his face acquiring a sudden expression of understanding. "Incidentally," he added, "isn't your paper a little too radical — one of those atheistic things? That's what I'm told. I don't read it myself though."

"But I look after its literary section only — miscellaneous articles, stories, reviews, poetry. Occasionally, I do a commentary myself on the cultural scene in Delhi. I wish you had seen my last piece on India's cultural heritage. Tolerance and non-violence. Almost a sermon."

"Sounds good." The bishop's face returned to its pristine glow as though some dark cobweb in his mind had been flicked

off. Then, after a pause, he added, "I'm happy you have decided to come to Christ voluntarily. Not many people do that,
you know. But I imagine your reason for the choice was . . . . "

Gautam had anticipated this question which Father Jones
found somewhat difficult to articulate. So he moved in promptly.

"It's not easy to explain, Father, these matters of the spirit.
Perhaps I should just say that I had felt it all these years —
this irrepressible urge to *be*. Maybe it had started with my
undergrad courses in literature, with my special interest in
Cardinal Newman — then Evelyn Waugh, Graham Greene,
Francois Mauriac . . . . "

Gautam felt very pleased to unreel a well-rehearsed speech.
He noticed that Father Jones had already lapped it all up.

"Yes, I understand," the bishop said, drawling out the last
word. Not that he had read any of these Catholic novelists.
Newman was the only one he really knew.

"And then," Gautam now warmed up, "look at what my
coreligionists are doing these days. All this pious talk about
Brahma, Ahimsa, Higher Self, cow protection, and then the
savage killing of innocent Muslims . . . Of course, Muslims
have done no better in Pakistan."

"All this is very sad."

"Very tragic. Don't you see, Father, that Christians alone
have kept their heads cool? . . . Well, I believe in Karma, concrete action — not just words, words?"

Suddenly Belinda, who had hunched up on the floor near
the bishop's chair, craned her neck forward and riveted her
deep burnt umber eyes on Gautam's face. For a moment he
thought as if this perceptive animal, and not the gullible bishop,
had seen through him.

"Yes," the bishop said thoughtfully, nodding.

A brief silence.

"But I hope you wouldn't mind waiting a couple of months,"
the bishop resumed. "I mean the usual initiation — Bible classes,
seminars and catechism. Sort of religious apprenticeship, you
know . . . Literature is one thing but the book of books is a
different undertaking altogether."

Gautam's face darkened. The mere thought of any more

delay agonized him. If only this man knew what he had already
been through. To hell with Hinduism, Islam or Christianity,
he said to himself — all that he wanted was an instant come-
off, a quick release, a snap way out of the labyrinth, a painless
deliverance.

"But haven't I already waited long enough, Father? What
about all those years of apprenticeship? I was hoping that I
would just knock at the door and it would be opened unto me."

He fired his first shot from the Bible.

"But haste in such matters, Mr. Mehta . . . " the bishop's
mind now slid over to another track. "In any case, shouldn't
you have brought your wife along too? It would have saved
time for both of you."

"Of course, I had thought of that. But, unfortunately, she
still seems to have some reservations. Her orthodox Hindu
background, I guess. But, Father, isn't the unbelieving wife
converted through her husband? That's clearly recognized in
Corinthians — isn't it?"

The bull's eye! Just the words! The bishop now realized
that the man knew his Bible, surely.

But Belinda, who had glided across the floor to the door,
shot another searching glance at Gautam. It was an uncanny
stare that almost chilled him.

"That's there, of course. But I should like to avoid any
discord in the family — as far as possible."

"No discord whatever," Gautam said, still under the eerie
spell of Belinda's gaze. "In fact, we have talked about this matter, and I feel she's coming around."

"Good."

"It's just that I shouldn't like to push . . . . "

"No coercions, please," Father Jones interjected. "We should
come to the Lord only out of the freedom and power of our
soul. Like you."

"Precisely."

Gautam turned to Belinda but she was now looking in-
tently at the aquarium. One goldfish was chasing another rather
furiously, stirring the placid water into mild ripples. The bishop
too appeared to be watching the fish-play but, in fact, his mind

was elsewhere. He was slowly swinging round to some snap decision.

"Well, if that's the case," he said, pulling out a deep breath, "we should perhaps go ahead without delay. I have no right to keep you away from the Lord." A pause. "How about next Sunday? We shall have a special service for you so that the entire congregation may bless you."

Gautam felt shocked to hear this. Any such public ceremony would be a disaster, he knew. Being a journalist, he knew the press would turn it on full blast, and someone would surely scent the whole thing. He had hoped for a quiet private ceremony, on a week day, with just one or two persons around. The certificate of baptism was all that he wanted to grab — his passport to freedom. But in spite of the bishop's disconcerting suggestion, he decided not to look ruffled up. This was the moment to keep cool.

"Certainly, Father. You may do it anytime, anyway . . . But I have always felt that true prayer is strictly a private affair, an intimate transaction between man and God — something articulated in the silence and tranquility of one's soul." Then, suddenly, Gautam brightened up as though some divine prompter had offered him the master cue. "I've just recalled something from *Matthew,* Father."

"What?"

"Yes," he said, pressing his forehead with his right hand as though he were extracting the exact words of the deep reservoir of his memory. "Yes," he repeated, "I've got the words — and when you pray, you must not be like the hypocrites, for they love to stand and pray in synagogues and at the street corners, that they may be seen by men . . . But when you pray, go into your room, and shut the door and pray to your Father who is in secret, and your Father who sees in secret will reward you." Gautam stopped for a moment, then rounded off smilingly: "I think I didn't miss a word."

"You certainly know your Bible intimately."

"I wonder. But this passage has been my favorite."

"That was a noble thought," the bishop said. "The Lord alone can look into the deepest recesses of our soul." His eyes then turned toward the aquarium.

Belinda slunk out of the room, as though crestfallen, for hadn't she lost some mysterious battle to Gautam?

The bishop now swivelled in his chair, took his diary out of the top drawer of his desk and said, "Will next Thursday be all right? We'll do it briefly and quietly."

"Thank you, Father."

"Of course, you'll have to bring someone along as your witness."

"Indeed, I do understand."

All that he wanted was a certificate of baptism to claim divorce from his wife. This was to be his passport to freedom — his release.

As he stood up to leave, an outburst of shouting blared in from the street. And then the noise of frenetic knocking at the main church gate, accompanied with harrowing cries for help. A menacing cry now slashed the air: "Kill him! Har Har Mahadev!" This was followed by another deafening shout — "Sat Sri Akal!"

Instantly, a group of church staff — junior priests, wardens and servants — ran into the courtyard. Father Jones and Gautam also rushed towards the gate which was being pounded by someone trying to crash through it. Then a head loomed just above it and a poignant cry exploded in the air — "Help me, please, h - e - l - p!" A man was struggling to scale the gate, but each time his head surfaced, his feet slipped and he sank to the ground. The steel gate stood firm and impregnable. Another heartrending shriek, then the sound of a body thudding.

By the time Father Jones and Gautam reached the gate, it was all over. As they opened it, there slumped on the floor the body of an old bearded man, riddled with stabs all over his chest, neck and abdomen. His penis had been chopped off, and his intestines lay sprawling around. His head was drenched in blood, and his hair looked like dry brittle grass. But his eyes were still open — in stark terror.

A few ring-leaders of this blood-thirsty mob looked momentarily at the bishop and then, as though overawed by the white dignity of this Englishman, they beckoned their followers to move on.

"Oh Jesus!" Father Jones exclaimed, as he crossed his chest with his right hand. "Is it another crucifixion?" he muttered in great anguish. Then, turning to Gautam, he added, "He knocked frantically for admittance, but we couldn't let him in."

"But would that have really helped? You are dealing with bloodhounds, not human beings."

"Maybe you're right." The bishop then looked at the dead body and said, "I wonder who this unfortunate creature is."

This prompted to action the bishop's servant, Samuel, who had stood around aghast like the others. Gently he pulled the body across the gate into the courtyard, turned it over, rummaged in the dead man's blood-stained clothes — and there came unstuck from one of his pockets a stamped, addressed envelope as though he had just stepped out to mail it. Samuel handed it over to his master, who opened it and passed it on to Gautam.

"Urdu, I guess," said the bishop. "Do you know this language?"

"Yes, Father."

The letter was addressed to Sultana Begum, wife of Abdul Mohammad, Mohalla Kashana, Aghapura, Allahabad. Gautam read out a quick rendition of the letter in English.

Dear Begum,

No trace of Haseena so far. I have been all over Delhi. Hindus and Sikhs are prowling around everywhere lusting for Muslim blood. I have to be wary because of my beard which attracts prying eyes everywhere. But so far Allah has been my protector.

This morning I talked to a Muslim shopkeeper in Urdu Bazar, near Jama Masjid. I was shocked to learn that most of the abducted girls from Allahabad, Lucknow and Patna have been brought to Delhi and forced into prostitution. O Allah! And in this nefarious immoral traffic, both Hindus and Muslims are operating as close accomplices. I shudder to think of our dear child.

Spent all morning in Jama Masjid — on my knees,

rubbing my nose against the sacred ground. Will Allah listen to my prayers?

Shall write to you tomorrow again, Insha-allah, after
meeting this shopkeeper. He has promised to put me on
to one of the leading pimps, Suleiman Ghani. I may have
to pay a heavy ransom to get her out if she is still alive
. . . Oh, these horrible imaginings! Don't let Salma stir out of
the Mohalla.

Sometimes I wonder why our British rulers chose to
leave us to these Hindu bloodsuckers.

God be with you all!

                                                        Abdul

The letter stunned Father Jones. He was so deeply moved
that he felt moisture welling up in his eyes. Was it all the
legacy of the Original Sin, he asked himself? Oh Christ, would
he be able to endure all this? Evil was rampant everywhere,
and there was no help.

"Will you write to his wife, please? Tell her . . . " But the
bishop's voice broke off; he felt a lump in his throat. He merely
looked away into blank space.

He was now lost in some deep thought. He had been in India
for only six months and had got embroiled in these cataclysmic
happenings. But, no, he wouldn't forsake his flock here. Hadn't
God preordained his staying on — to do his duty unto Christ?
If he too ran away with his other compatriots, who would re-
claim lost souls like Mehta's?

As Father Jones stood there transfixed, deeply immersed in
his thoughts, Gautam kept gazing at the dead man whose face
had acquired a new eloquence in the light of his poignant letter.
Suddenly he recognized a striking resemblance between Mohammad and his own father — except, of course, the beard.
The same freckled face, narrow forehead, heavy chin, thick-set
jaw, sharp nose and round shoulders. He felt the pull of some
mysterious bond, an irresistible tug at his heart-strings.

"So it hasn't turned out to be a calm day, after all," Father
Jones mumbled, almost in a self-derisive tone.

"No."

"How sadly mistaken we both were."

"Yes, Father."

"And this may well be the beginning of another round of violence."

"Most likely. I think there'll be a quick and bloody retaliation."

Again the bishop looked at the dead man, and asked Gautam: "Shouldn't we inform the police?"

"But would it serve any purpose? I'm certain they are in league with these murderers. They move in only after the event. They are like the Roman gladiators; they take these killings as a great sport — a source of entertainment."

"Then there's no law and order."

"No. Delhi's only hope is William Thornton, our Commissioner of Police. But what can a single man do?"

"Thornton — is he English?" Father Jones asked.

"No, Anglo-Indian. Father English, mother Kashmiri."

"I see," the bishop murmured. "I'm glad you were with me this afternoon."

"But do you realize, Father, what *you* are doing for me?"

"I don't know. Let Christ be with you hereafter — let him guide your steps." Then, after a moment's reflection, he added, "Be careful, Mr. Mehta, as you go home. There's madness on the streets."

"No harm will come to me since I live in a Hindu locality."

"That's good . . . Then until Thursday!"

The bishop now turned to Samuel and asked him to have the dead body removed for a quiet burial in the backyard of the church.

As Gautam walked out of the churchyard onto the street, he was surprised to see all quiet everywhere. Where had the rioters disappeared? Gone underground? Had they been warned by the police to stay away for a short while so that law might stage a sham investigation into the incident?

Once out on the street a gelid sensation gripped him. What if he was ambushed by Muslims! Hindus, he knew, wouldn't harm him for circumcision was the litmus test for both the warring communities to ascertain an individual's identity.

He kept walking on, engrossed in these thoughts. Down the lane, all the Tibetan vendors had already folded up their stalls and were gone. The entire place had been taken over by armed policemen who moved about cockily, brandishing their neatly polished batons.

Near Red Fort there was no taxi, only a solitary tonga, with a hefty Sikh driver perched on the front seat. Gautam thought it safer to ride in this vehicle, with a sturdy Sardar as his escort.

"Can you take me to Darya Ganj, Hindu Sector, please?"

The driver shot a quick glance at Gautam.

"Yes, but only via the Jumna route. I think there's trouble near the southern end of Faiz Bazaar."

Gautam knew it was only a ruse to touch him for more money.

"All right?"

"Ten rupees."

"Let's go."

As the rickety vehicle, pulled by a shaggy horse, jerked into a noisy rattle on the road, the driver started up conversation presumably as a palliative for the exorbitant fare he had hooked out of his passenger.

"Are you a refugee from Pakistan, sir?"

"Yes, from Lahore."

"Lost everything?"

"Only property — my family came through intact."

"Were you with your family in Lahore, sir?"

"No, I had come to Delhi a couple years ago."

"Lucky. My family had the worst of it all. Two of my sisters were carried away. My old man's throat was slit before my mother's eyes — then he was roasted alive. I was the only one to escape. Oh, these blasted Muslims!"

"Sorry to hear this."

"But we got one Muslim this afternoon, near St. John's. An old bearded fellow. That was a good catch."

"Yes, I know."

Gautam wondered if the Sardar had himself been one of the killers.

Five Protest Poems from the 1975-77 Emergency

During 1975-77, 110,000 people were imprisoned under Maintenance of Internal Security acts and Defense of India rules which do not require warrants, trial, or habeas corpus generally.

No Troublemaker

NAGARJUNA

You were no troublemaker
You did not wish to start a fire, you
Did not carry a rag soaked in oil or a hand grenade
Concealed within the folds of your sari.
You did not distribute naughty pamphlets on poverty,
You did not even have a Neem stick on you,
For scrubbing your teeth.

Hai Ram, you had just gone for a dip in the Holy Ganges,
And were bringing back
Merely your dripping laundry and a pot
Of the holy waters, home.

How could you have annoyed the Border Security Forces?

Hai Ram, and you end up with a bullet in your thigh.

She, at whose commands
The wheels of this kingdom grind
Is a woman too.
But she shall not visit you at the hospital.
An ordinary woman's thigh is not a B.S.F. checkpost,
And neither are you the widow of a martyr
That she should come
And shake hands with you.

Translated from the Hindi by Mrinal Parde

Two Poems

A Song

Kill them
Burn them—
They eat what we grow
drink what we labor
yet they keep us out
calling us untouchables
They let in the dog that eats our shit
but bar us from their doors
They have their gods in every lane
yet they brag that God is one
They call us Harijans—
"God's chillun"—
and keep us from school and temple
to slave for them in farms and fields.
Kill them
Burn them
Flay them alive these whoresons!

Translated from the Kannada by P. Rama Moorthy

I Must Have A Word

I must have a word
with cactuses and thorny plants.
I must put a question
to the moon
whose light is stolen.
I must free
the blood-red roses
from their thorns.

Wells without water,
shameless politicians,
cops who move

with clubs
like thorny bushes,
Oh world,
I must have words with you.

We must speak
while there may be time
to grow the color green again
in this, our world,
daily done to death,
our mountains trucked away,
our clinging grass
plucked up, the desert sands
allotted all the land
as if in triplicate,
passed on by bureaucrats,
who take the bribes of winds.

And each branch burns now
along with the voice of reason,
allowed to wither,
held in jails, barred
like woodsheds.
                        All the great
fruits wither, mango,
jack-fruit, wisdom of the ages,
the soft plum of gentleness.
Oh world, I must stop you,
We must have words, and now.

Translated and adapted from the Kannada by Sumatheendra
Nadig and David Ray

A Poster

Kumar Vikal

It's harmless enough,
merely a government poster,
like a painting that's holy,
to be worshipped by masses.
Read it, the voice of the gods,
conveying the message,
statistics, thousands
of promises. Read it,
help spread the word,
how our prestige has gone up,
how prices have fallen,
how the World Bank has sanctioned
an enormous loan, then another,
all for our industry,
linked to fabulous employment.
And all this generates millions,
rupees recycled
into ever new glories.
Think of the profits,
ripe as a harvest.
Then we'll build houses.
The poor shall have shelter.
No more sleeping in gutters,
no more love on the sidewalks.
Let the wretched shout out
Jai Hind! Hallelujah!
But between you and me,
the poor man's afraid, afraid
to stand there and read,
afraid to read. And, my friend,
if the poor can't read
and can't write, why bother
to print all these posters?
Why bother to promise him?
Why bother to notice him?

Translated and adapted from the Hindi by
Mrinal Parde and David Ray

A Poem Smuggled Out Of Prison

JYOTIRMOY DATTA

Jail handicrafts are no longer what they used to be!
We do not cut diamonds nor polish rubies.
The silk woven in Ward Thirteen
Was fit for even a Chinese queen.
Indeed, for the wedding of Princess Alexandra, Bengal's gift
Was a durbar scene done in gold by a blind convict.

It is but natural that the most seductive wedding veils
Shall be the produce of the midnight looms of repressed males.

The loveliest roses of the Governor's annual flower show
Always came from the condemned prisoners' row.
Perhaps that is one of the reasons
The only cheerful poems these days come out of prisons.

Translated from the Bengali by the author

This Man

G. S. Shivarudrappa

His cauldrons seethe.
In the nest of the heart
they rick:
a wreckage of clocks.

A hundred bogeys
shuttle night and day
upon these rails.

These are the noises; and then
the silence.

Light and dark goad him
as they run.
The embered east, and night
as she unfurls her parasol
of a million holes, and that flood
of sighs we call the wind,
all these run over him
without pity, without end.

Circuses, movies, restaurants,
acrobatic shows,
cigarettes, cards, snake-charming
feats, poetry circles, and the high falutin
of endless talks,
all that feast of myth and legend:
these, and such as these,
are placebos for his pain.
From the cracks in his ceiling
stream the rains, the thoughts,
and muddy the floors. But
green are the shoots of desire.

Still, despair
does not drown him,
he does not curse his gods,

but bears like a patient pole
a light upon his head.
His silence, a fire, keeps a vigil
in corruption's wakes and fairs . . . .

Translated from the Kannada by A. K. Ramanujan

Stormward

SATI KUMAR

I have turned my face
stormward.

Uprooted they lie,
forests, men, direction, signs
and all.

The brown desert of cultures
rises up in the storm
and shattering me passes away.

I wish to see the storm's face
and that is why
I have turned my face stormward.

But in the lashes of storm
nothing is visible—
eyes are flickering, bloodshot

But to turn my face back from the storm—
for that I no longer have the courage.

Translated from the Punjabi by Manohar Bandhyopadhyay

Two Poems

GORDON KORSTANGE

Murugesan's Daughter

for Rathanam

A lady, yes
like a real white lady
trying on a new hat
she gingerly lifts the brass pot
with two slender dark hands
onto her poised head
and looking into the clear mirror
of her body
she tilts it this way
                    and that
until it fits,
                then
infinitely pleased with herself,
and infinitely more wonderful
than any lady in any hat,
she puts another brass pot
on top of that.

Let Them Eat Children

Such long black hair the women weave and braid
And let down to wash at the temple pond
Where they laugh and splash in the cool water,
Then fill their pots and hoist them on their heads
To walk dripping down the dusty street
And sit beside their house and pick the lice
From that mass of dark hair never to be cut
But for the god upon the sacred hill
And never to be loosed but for their lord's
Desire at night upon the marriage mat.

Such love they bear their boggle-eyed babies
Propped and bared to the mad, staring world

Astride broad goddess hips where they watch
Warily the big hands that poke and paw
And suffer the probing grip of grasping love
That planted them into this burning world
To feel the first blasts of biting need
That bear them back and forth from hand to arm
To hungering mouth and then again to sit
Upon the firm perch of their mother's hip.

Such rags they wear, the big-eyed scrawnies,
Frayed and torn as wind-whipped fronds,
Worn on brown skin smooth as river rock;
They meander along beneath bright sun
Behind delicate cattle's bony bulk
Toward the fields that keep their hunger safe
In ancient lowly motion's aching arms;
Toward the empty, sun-worn fields that hug
The sleeping village through the pit of night
And bear the seed the goddess blessed with hope.

Such stares they stare of star-eyed wonder,
Sitting on the moonlit village sand,
At the loud threats of blustering big demons
Who dare to war upon the strutting gods
Until they strangle tight the helpless earth
In their wild struggle for the juice of life,
Above the darkened village they rage and roar,
Ready to throttle the audacious deeds of men
Who try to leave their humbling mother's arms.
Such terror they bear, the children,
                              such terror,
                                    such love.

The Ghost of the Unborn

PRASANNA KUMAR MISHRA

All your breasts
overflow with milk.
Overbrimmed pitchers, spilling water,
Mothers! You'll pass this way!
On this path, from the river.
Dripping milk, you'll pass by,
drop by drop

Mother died unable to give birth to me,
I died without being born.

Same womb, same flower, same pain,
and the accumulated milk meant for me, dying;
now in this tree like an unseen bird
I perch, oh mother!

Like you, too my mother
used to fetch water from the river,
I could have been born from your womb too,
I too could have been cradled in your arms,
I too could have suckled your breasts,
and I too could have been the star of your eye.

But I have no lips,
and thirst cries on only for milk.

This way you will, always pass by, oh mothers
I could have been your child too.

Translated from the Oriya by Jayanta Mahapatra

A Naked Stick in the Matchbox

HARIBHAJAN SINGH

Mid day
A crowded street
A house all by itself
Scorching sun
Breathless wind

Danger without a cause
Wish I could not go to sleep
Heart startles into a beat
The house like a matchbox
He puts it into his pocket

House in his pocket
He walks away to the city
Fast and brisk
A bare lonely stick in the box
I go on throbbing fast and loud
Pregnant with a live fire

This other woman's man will take away my naked self out
And make me look all the more naked
Burn with my own light as I would

Nothing has happened
House all by itself
Bolted from within
Scorching sun
Breathless wind
I lie in the dark
Uncared for
Unable to go to sleep.

Translated from the Punjabi by Gulzar Singh Sandhu

Urban Expansion

MAJID AMJAD

They who have stood at the gate of this singing stream for
    twenty years
Elegant sentinels at the borders of rolling fields
Agreeably dark, shade-sprinkling, fruit-laden, tall
For twenty thousand were sold away all the verdurous trees
    They whose every gusty breath was strange magic
    Murderous axes came and split the bodies of those heroes
Down with a thud fell the blue wall of wounded trees
Huge bodies being sawn, falling skeletons, leaf and fruit being
    cut away
Heaps of dead bodies in the pale shroud of trembling sunlight
Today standing beside the gate of this singing stream I think
    In this shambles my thought is the only flowering branch
    Now, O children of Adam, a mortal blow for me too.

Translated from Urdu by S. R. Faruqi and F. W. Pritchett

Plunder Blunder

RAJ CHENGAPPA

New Delhi, March 2001. On the forty-fourth floor of an apartment complex, in Room 4407, six-year-old Preeti sat on a plastic chair watching a television program. The room around her was made entirely of plastic: doors, windows, beds, chairs. Preeti's mother bent over a pot of stew on a solar stove, in which cacti curry bubbled: their daily staple, boiled, fried or raw.

The geography lesson had begun on television. There were very few schools left and teaching was mostly done on television. Only the affluent could send their children to school: a notebook cost Rs 60 and a textbook, made from precious yellow paper, more than Rs 200. On the screen the teacher was explaining the physical features of India. According to him, the country was divided into three types of terrain: barren hills and mountains, huge swamps and vast stretches of desert. The biggest swamp in the north was the Indo-Gangetic Swamp and in the south the Cauvery Swamp. While the Himalayas were very high "rocky" mountains marked with steep ravines and gullies, the Vindhyas and the Western Ghats were huge sandy dunes dotted occasionally by cacti. India was now called a tropical desert swamp.

Twenty years ago, said the teacher, India was filled with lovely green forests, the sweetest of fruits and the healthiest of pulses but all the forests had been cut down and desert had crept over the fields. Preeti was looking disbelievingly at the television so her mother decided that she would take her to the museum nearby where they displayed apples, oranges and other

*fruits. But the visit would have to be next week because Preeti
was supposed to take her monthly bath: there was no point in
taking her out to be covered with dust.*

*Moreover, a sandstorm seemed to be building up. Preeti's
mother looked out of the window. Delhi looked like a concrete
jungle. Trees which once shaded the avenues were things of the
past and only an endless row of high-rise buildings was visible.
Not far from where Preeti stayed, Baldev Singh and his family
watched the approaching sandstorm fearfully from their ram-
shackle hut. Baldev Singh had brought his family to this meager
shelter after the giant Gangetic Swamp swallowed up his fertile
land years ago.*

*In fact all the farmers had migrated to the city as their
fields had long since turned barren. Now they lived in millions
of huts that had cropped up on the outskirts of Delhi. While
those in the high-rise buildings were safer, the hut dwellers
were under the constant threat of being swamped by sandstorms
that frequently and regularly swept through Delhi, or of being
drowned in the occasional floods. Delhi had become a con-
gested and dusty city, with a population of 20 million. It was
the same for all the other cities in India.*

Apocalyptic as the preceding scenario may appear, the threat
is frighteningly real. Deforestation's relentless march is steadily
stripping the country bare of its forest cover, leaving behind
barren man-made deserts. From the majestic coniferous forests
of the Himalayas to the deciduous belt of the Vindhyas and the
tropical evergreen canopy over the Western Ghats, the story
is tragically the same; indiscriminate destruction of forests that
could eventually turn India into a vast and inhospitable wasteland.

In his dingy office in the bowels of Krishi Bhavan in New
Delhi, Narain Bachkheti, the bespectacled inspector-general of
forests, peers gloomily at a pile of charts showing the damage
done by deforestation so far. "Experts recognize three different
stages in the march of man; civilization dominated by forests,

civilization overcoming forests, and civilization dominating forests," he says, "our country is now passing through an acute phase of the third stage which is civilization dominating forests to the point of destroying them and destroying itself in the process. This is not an empty threat."

The danger, in fact, is far more. The Union Government's Forest Department estimates that within the last three decades, 4.5 million hectares of forests or an area the size of Tamil Nadu, have vanished, leaving behind barren land. The national forest policy of 1952 envisaged the country's forest cover being raised from 23 per cent to 33 per cent of the total land area. Three decades later, it has been reduced to an ecologically mind-boggling 10 per cent. Every year, lush green forests the size of New Delhi, Bombay and Calcutta combined are being devastated with criminal abandon, leaving behind the seeds of a future disaster that is Orwellian in its magnitude. (The varied climatic zones of the country such as the warm, humid climate of the west coast to the hot desert of the Rajasthan and the cold Himalayan ranges have endowed India with a fascinating biological diversity. There are an estimated 13,000 plant species and 65,000 species of animals in the country. India harbors 5.2 per cent of the plant and 4.3 per cent of the animal species in the world.)

Currently, only five out of India's 22 states (Himachal, Orissa, Tripura, Madhya Pradesh and Assam) come anywhere near the desirable one-third land area under forest cover. Further, most states exist in the bliss of ignorance. Orissa, for instance, stoutly insists that 43.6 per cent of its land area is forested while satellite pictures taken six years ago clearly show that the actual figure is an ecologically insufficient 30.1 per cent. Other states are no less culpable:

Himachal Pradesh's forest area is a mere 19 per cent compared to the official claim of 39.1 per cent with the giant deodars in the famed Kulu valley having become virtually extinct. An estimated Rs 50 crore worth of trees each year are the victims of illegal felling by contractors who smuggle the precious timber to the ravenous wood industries of the plains.

In Uttar Pradesh, satellite pictures show the towering Himalayas stripped bare of their thick coniferous cover to a height of almost 2,800 meters—the limit of year-round human habitation.

Madhya Pradesh, which boasts of the largest forest belt in the country (16.6 million hectares) has lost more than two million hectares of teak, sal and bamboo forests; the largest amount of forest cover lost by any single state.

In Assam, another forest-rich state, only 23.03 per cent of reserve forests have survived the combined onslaught of 380 forest-based industries including 40 plywood factories and 10 paper mills. Official statistics, however, still blissfully maintain that 39.2 per cent of the area is under forest cover.

In Karnataka, the mangrove forests along the west coast have all but disappeared, the scrub forests of the Deccan plateau denuded and the evergreen forests reduced to a paltry 5 per cent from the original 20 per cent.

Maharashtra projects a sorrier picture with vast areas, particularly in Ratnagari district, having been laid bare of forest cover.

West Bengal has lost 3.2 lakh hectares of its forest in the past 30 years.

The brutal rape of India's forests has raised the curtain on a man-made ecological catastrophe of unprecedented magnitude which, in its ultimate effect, could threaten life more climatically than the combined fury of all natural disasters. The destruction of forests is relentlessly transforming all mountains and hills into uncontrollable barren landslide zones. It threatens to convert the country's fertile river basins into unproductive swamps. It is pulling the deadening desert zones over green agricultural lands. It is incessantly adding to the unending flood of rural migrants to overcrowded towns and urban conglomerates. It is making maneaters out of tigers and rogues out of elephants. It is fast threatening to take India to an unenviable era where not only food will be scarce but there will not be fuel to cook it. A somber Prime Minister Mrs. Indira Gandhi told foresters in Dehra Dun recently: "If we care for our future we must save our forests."

Balance Destroyed

In more specific terms, the galloping destruction of the country's forests has succeeded in overturning the delicate ecological balance between soil and vegetation, ushering in attendant dangers. The thick canopy of overgrowth in tropical forests acts as rainbreakers, reducing the damage to the topsoil. With deforestation, the rich topsoil is washed away by torrential rain, leaving barren land and a high rate of siltation in river beds. For instance, owing to the denudation in the north-eastern hills of Arunachal Pradesh, the bed of the Brahmaputra river has risen by as much as 14 feet, increasing the danger of floods.

B.B. Vohra, chairman of the National Committee for Environment Planning (NCEP) a body that advises the Government on environmental policies, estimates that every year, 6,000 million tons of topsoil, equivalent in nutrients to twice the annual production of fertilizer, is washed away, resulting in a loss of around Rs 1,000 crore. It has reduced 7 percent of the country's cultivable land to barrenness or an area capable of producing half the country's annual foodgrain requirement. Two years ago, Vohra assessed that it would cost at least Rs 50,000 crore—half the entire public sector outlay in the Sixth Plan—to put the country's land and forests back in order.

The grim statistics march through countless reports and surveys like the swathes of bare land left behind by deforestation. The Birla-funded Economic and Scientific Research Foundation estimates that out of a total of 306 million hectares of cultivable land, 145 million hectares or 45 per cent of the land area is seriously threatened with erosion and is desperately in need of soil and water conservation measures, as is at least a quarter of the entire forest area in the country. Soil erosion and high siltation in river beds have jeopardized no less than 39 major river valley projects which generate more than half the country's power requirements and irrigate one-quarter of its total food crops. Says well-known zoologist Satish Chandran of Trivandrum: "The entire ecological system is disintegrating. Some of the areas look like Hiroshima after the blast."

The National Commission on Floods estimates that the area

vulnerable to floods has doubled from 20 million hectares to 40 million hectares. Last year, a total of 10 states experienced devastating floods in which 1,181 people and 58,000 head of cattle perished. The total annual loss due to floods averages out at an estimated Rs 800 crore.

Floods

Siltation in river beds has reached disastrous proportions. The Brahmaputra bed has risen by 14 feet. The Jhelum in Kashmir has overflowed its banks in 13 years out of 20 and the probability of floods in Kashmir valley was found to be as high as 70 per cent. In Bhakra and Ramganga reservoirs the rate of siltation was estimated to be one and a half times the assumed rate. "At the explosive rate of sedimentation there will hardly be any Himalayan reservoir left and the whole irrigation and power system in the Indo-Gangetic plain will be jeopardized," warns Professor S.L. Shah, emeritus scientist of the Vivekananda Laboratory of Hill Agriculture, Almora.

"We are heading for an ecological disaster," warns Nalni Jayal, joint secretary, Department of Environment (DOE). The DOE is a classic example of the Government agencies involved with the problems of deforestation. When the DOE was formed two years ago, it was hailed optimistically as the Government's trouble-shooting agency entrusted with the task of ending mindless deforestation. But so far it has done precious little, as officials like Jayal admit, and is still in the process of "organizing itself." The department incredibly, has so far been given no terms of reference and is currently showing signs of being slowly strangled by the bureaucratic noose. A state forest official, when asked about the DOE's contribution to deforestation, quipped derisively: "Haven't you heard? They're busy studying deforestation in Antarctica."

The DOE is not the only agency at which accusing fingers are being pointed. The NCEP has been largely dispensing advice that nobody listens to. Says one ecologist: "The NCEP has no eyes to see and no arms to work. It concentrates on dishing out advice that nobody wants to eat." Similarly, the Forest Research Institute in Dehra Dun, the country's premier institution, proudly claims that its most significant achievement has been forestry product research, an area that directly benefits industry, the indirect cause of deforestation. In fact, K.M. Tewari, its greyhaired president, admits candidly that the institute has not made a single study on the total impact of deforestation. Most ecologists and conservationists unanimously agree that the Central Government agencies are predominantly populated by people living in ecological ivory towers, who readily admit to the plethora of problems but seem to provide few or no answers. (As regards conservation measures, most of the 19 national parks and 202 wildlife sanctuaries covering an area of 75,763 square kilometers, or 2.3 per cent of the country's geological area, were unfortunately the former hunting preserves of feudal lords and princes. These parks or sanctuaries are designed to conserve the more spectacular animals such as the tiger or elephant and give no importance to the preservation of the overall biological diversity. To this day India has not established a biosphere reserve although 40 countries including Sri Lanka, Pakistan, Nigeria, Iran, and Bulgaria have set up 161 reserves throughout the world.)

Bungling

The next rung of the ecological ladder, the state forest departments, have done more bungling than jungling. According to ecologists, the forest departments have laid the basic foundations of deforestation by hiring contractors indiscriminatingly to exploit forest resources. Once the foothold was secured, the contractors indulged in an orgy of forest destruction, with the forest department actively conniving in the illegal felling, which has now grown to alarming proportions. Even a large percentage of reserve forests which are labelled as "virgin forests" by the department, have been raped systematically by unscrupulous contractors with a share of the "profits" going to bribery-prone forest officials. In Uttar Pradesh at least a quarter of its rich forest area has been lost by illegal felling, and state Forest Minister Nirbhay Naraian Singh admits that even today illegal felling is rampant in the Nainital district. In the Himalayan belt, contractors hired to tap resin have been over-exploiting the trees, while forest guards look the other way, leading to the death of thousands of mature trees.

The merchants' role played by the forest departments has come under severe criticism from ecologists. Said one of them: "The forest department concentrates on the price tags of species. They behave like middlemen. Middlemen are susceptible to pressures and cuts. Basically all foresters are becoming agriculturists and they may as well hand it over to sardars who would do a better job of it."

The contractor system has other invisible evils as well. Contractors rarely hire local tribals who inhabit the forests but instead bring in work gangs from outside. This not only isolates the tribals but allows the work gangs to intrude into the forests. Currently, tribals in Madhya Pradesh are being hired by contractors to collect sal seeds. They are paid Rs 50 a quintal while the contractors sell it for Rs 250 a quintal. They pay the Government a royalty of Rs 30 a quintal and pocket the rest.

Says Madhav Gadgil, eminent ecologist from the Indian Institute of Science in Bagalore: "The entire problem is that there are three segments of people dealing with forests: the local population, government and the industries, all three of whom have no personal stake in it at all. The local population is not bothered about preserving forests because they earn more if they steal the wood instead of working for low wages. The industry is interested only in immediate profits. The bureauracy has neither responsibility nor accountability. An officer never spends more than two years in a particular area. As a result nobody sheds any tears when forests are destroyed."

In 1971, after the national commission on agriculture urged forest departments to be more "productive," a total of 18 states esablished forest development corporations to develop monoculture plantations for commercial use. Typically, instead of locating the plantations in areas of spare cover, the corporations have been busy clearing dense forests to make way for the plantations and showing the timber sold as profits. In the Markhanda area of Chandrapur district of Maharashtra, existing forests have been registered as "miscellaneous" and deliberately destroyed to make way for eucalyptus trees. Out of 1.4 lakh trees planted, only 40 survive today. Only recently has the Central Government issued instructions to state governments to stop clear-felling of forests and locate the plantations on already deforested land.

Much of the problem, however, stems from the fact that forests were a state subject till 1976 when it was transferred to the concurrent list under the 42nd Amendment. As a result, while the Central Government laid down the national forest policy, which was more pontifical than specific, the states have largely paid contemptuous heed to the Center's directives and proceeded to decimate forests almost at will. In the Kali hydel project area in Karnataka, for instance, entire forests have been submerged and the people displaced by the project were given alternative plots in Ramnagaram, where another forest belt was destroyed to rehabilitate the people.

This kind of bureaucratic bungling and dabbling causing irreversible loss continues to plague the country. Till recently the cost-benefit analysis done to study the viability of a river valley project never took cognizance of the ecological damage. In the Himalayas pylons were rammed into the ground with no thought of the landslides they would cause. As a result, in the hill districts of Uttar Pradesh vast stretches of fertile land have been covered by rubble dislodged by the pylons to the valleys below.

The forest department takes refuge behind the most obvious reason for deforestation: population increase. Bachkheti points out that while India has 2 per cent of the earth's land area and 1 per cent of its productive forests the country has 15 per cent of the world's human population and 10 per cent of its cattle population. With an annual population rise of 23 million people, forests the size of Rajasthan have been encroached upon for. cultivation. Excessive browsing and grazing have thinned forests too. The country's livestock population of 400 million estimatedly graze on 11 per cent of the total forest area.

Scarcities

Meanwhile, fuel wood and industrial wood are in short supply because of the failure of the forest department to preserve existing forests or re-stock them. India's forests are cur-

rently only able to provide 20 million cubic meters out of the
165 million cubic meters of firewood required by the country's
rural population. An FAO (Food and Agricultural Organization)
expert has estimated that by the turn of the century, India will
be able to grow enough food but will not have enough firewood
to cook it.

Industrial wood faces the same shortage problem. Of the
total demand of 26 million tons, forests could only provide
11 million tons. By the end of the century, the demand is
likely to be around 65 million tons. "We may not even have
enough wood to manufacture paper or furniture in the next
20 years," warns a forest official.

To combat the fuel and fodder crisis, the Government is
now flourishing its social forestry scheme as the panacea for
the ailment that afflicts Indian forests. The scheme envisages
the growing of trees in village woodlots, wasteland and degraded
forests. One hundred districts have so far been selected to raise
firewood plantations over an area of 2.6 lakh hectares. An estimated 580 million seedlings will be distributed to villagers.
Meanwhile, 12 states have already launched their own social
forestry schemes with the financial aid of the World Bank and
the Swedish Government. Judging by current performances, the
scheme will prove a dismal failure unless it is overseen adequately and strict controls imposed.

According to a study done by the Indian Institute of Man-
agement, Bangalore, Kolar district in Karnataka offers an excellent example of misguided enthusiasm in the social forestry
concept. In this district, farmers have replaced food crops with
eucalyptus plantations to sell to textile mills in the state. The
result is that food production has dropped dramatically. Neither
is eucalyptus suitable for firewood or fodder. Most ecologists
dismiss social forestry as a "numbers game" in which meaning-
less statistics are bandied about with no relevance to the problem.

Sundarlal Bahuguna, leader of the Chipko Andolan, a movement to save trees, reads a dire conspiracy in the social forest
program of the Government whom he accuses of encouraging
common-culture species to meet the rayon and wood needs of
developed countries. Queries the bearded Bahuguna: "Are we

going to use our land for the short-term exploitation of a few affluent countries or are we going to make our country self-sufficient in food and clothing?"

Neither is the Center unaware of the problem. The Government has under proposal the All India Forest Act but even this has been the target of criticism by ecologists. Their main fear is that it serves to give immense power to the states by widening the definition of forests to include any land so notified by the forest department. It also proposes to increase the imprisonment term for offenders from six months to three years and fines from Rs 500 to Rs 5,000, and empower forest officers or police to arrest without magisterial order, any person against whom there is reasonable suspicion of violating the act. But this, ecologists feel, will only succeed in increasing corruption in the department. Says Nair: "The bill will provide an army of guards to protect forests. But you cannot preserve forests with bayonets. People have to preserve forests."

Tribals' Protest

Ironically, that is precisely what is happening. Angered by governmental indifference and the ruthless exploitation of forests, anti-deforestation movements, mainly among tribals, has been making a significant impact on the forestry scene. In Chamouli and Tehri districts, the famous Chipko movement which employs the technique of clinging to trees to save them from indiscriminate axes, has been rapidly gaining in strength and support. Apart from having saved thousands of trees, they have forced the Uttar Pradesh Government to ban the felling of trees above 3,800 feet.

In the Chotanagpur area of Bihar, tribals have been waging a three-year-old battle to prevent commercial teak from replacing sal forests. Bastar tribals have had equal success with preventing a pine plantation which would have replaced their sal forests. Ecological movements like Seva the Silent Valley movement in Kerala, the Bedthi agitation in Karnataka and the Bhoomi Seva movement in Maharashtra have made their own contribution.

The Silent Valley, a five million year-old virgin tropical forest, would have been destroyed if the Kerala Government had gone ahead and built the Rs 72 crore hydroelectric project. But faced with a sustained agitation by ecologists which earned worldwide support, the Government was forced to appoint an expert committee to review the viability of the project. The fate of Silent Valley still hangs in the balance, like the rest of India's forests.

Meanwhile, the increasing alienation of the tribals in these areas is sowing its own seeds of discontent and many experts grimly predict open revolt in some areas. Says well-known journalist B. G. Verghese: "We must let tribals become part-ners in forest production and not merely dismiss them with compensations. They are in an explosive mood and movements like Jharkhand are not secessionist movements but an ex-pression of anger and frustration. Our policy should be tribals and development and not tribals or development."

The consensus emerging among ecologists and more sensi-tive elements in the Government is that instead of handing over the responsibility of afforestation and conservation entirely to the forest department, the local population, including the tribals, should be largely involved in future forestry schemes. Instead of handing over tapping of forest resources to contractors or even to forest development corporations, the people around these forests should be employed to do it so that they would more readily preserve their forests when their livelihood depends on it. For afforestation programs the vast stretches of degraded forest and revenue land lying fallow should be handed over to local popu-lations for growing trees (with the help of government finance) and reaping a share of the yield. Not only will they guard these trees from indiscriminate felling but insure that these survive the vagaries of weather. Said an ecologist optimistically: "By these measures we may not be able to get back our original forests but at least we will be able to halt further devastation of our forests."

Some semblance of a start has been made in Orissa and Gujarat where tribals are being trained in advanced methods of tree culture and being paid wages during training. After the

training, they are given land to plant trees and the eventual produce belongs to them. But these states are only two faint glim-
mers of light in an area of almost total darkness. The main fear,
says an ecologist, is that the country could easily turn into one
vast desert before the real impact of deforestation dawns on the
people and the policy makers.

Nature's Bounty

The roots of trees act like a sponge absorbing rainwater and
releasing the excess in a controlled manner, insuring a measured
flow to the river. The roots also bind the soil and the humus.
The dense canopy of the foliage breaks the force of the fiercest of
rainstorms and allows the water to fall as gentle drops to the
ground.

Denuded hills cause floods, because the lack of vegetation
means an excessive run-off of water to the plains below. In
summer, on the other hand, there is an acute shortage of water
because the underground storage system has not been adequately
charged and this often leads to drought. And with nothing to
hold it in place, the precious top-soil which takes 600 years to
form is washed down rendering entire hillsides barren and causing river-beds to silt up. Landslides become a regular feature.

Trees also shelter and feed many animals and birds. They
help to purify the atmosphere by absorbing carbon dioxide and
converting it into oxygen. It is estimated that one tree produces as much oxygen as is needed by 200 people in the same
period. Trees also reduce noise pollution in cities and check the
heat build-up in the atmosphere by preventing heat from radiat-
ing into it from bare surfaces.

The greenery is also known to provide protection for the
eyes. A study conducted in Bombay revealed that on a hot afternoon asphalt reflects 45 per cent of the incident light while
foliage reflects only 9 per cent.

To sum up, forests help in no small measure to manage the
environment. From which the saying: forests precede civilization
and deserts follow.

A Double-edged Sword

In the wake of the reckless deforestation two unique but violently opposite popular movements have bubbled. While in the Chamouli and Tehri districts of Uttar Pradesh the now famous Chipko volunteers are out to save trees and grow them, in the Singhbhum district of Bihar tribals have organized themselves into a "Jungle Katao" movements and have been felling trees in protest.

The Chipko movement was formed in dramatic circumstances in Gopeshwar, the picturesque headquarters of Chamouli, 450 km from New Delhi. In 1979 when the Uttar Pradesh Government auctioned ash trees to an Allahabad sports manufacturer they alloted the same forest area where just a month ago a request by the local people to cut the wood was turned down by it.

Angered by the Government's action the villagers decided on a unique protest: when the contractor came to fell the trees the villagers gathered around and hugged the trees. Thus Chipko, which means hug in Hindi, was born. The movement was co-ordinated by a Sarvodaya organization called the Dasholi Gram Swarajya Sangh headed by the rugged Chandi Prasad Bhatt.

While initially it began for economic reasons the movements took an ecological turn after the bearded Sundarlal Bahuguna, a Gandhian living in neighboring Tehri, took active interest in it. With a band of enthusiasts he set out on his famous Kashmir to Kohima trek and his reports exposed the reckless deforestation that was taking place in the Himalayas.

Increased Awareness

Wherever Bahuguna tramped he educated people about the need to preserve trees and the dangers that would befall them if they did not. The sustained agitation by Chipko volunteers forced the Uttar Pradesh to ban felling of trees in hill areas. Said Bahuguna: "Our movement is not just for saving the hills: it is for the survival of mankind."

In Chamouli, curiously it is the women who are the main force of the Chipko movement. The burden of gathering firewood falls on them and every year the search takes longer. Said 65-year-old Paravati Devi, her face lined with toil and age: "It takes me at least the whole day to collect firewood. We must preserve our trees." Not only this, the village now seems to have an increased awareness that trees prevent landslides and floods. Last year the villagers started their afforestation program and have so far planted 3 lakh seedlings on village commons. They also hold eco-development camps to educate the people from the surrounding villages about the need of forest preservation.

Destructive Anger

But in Bihar the reverse is taking place. The Jungle Katao movement began in Singhbhum in 1977 when the Bihar Forest Development Corporation decided to replace the natural sal forests with the highly priced teak. The tribals depended on sal not only for food but also for agricultural implements, as well as employment. After repeated requests to the Government had failed, the tribals, under the banner of Jharkhand, an age-old Marxist-led movement for the establishment of a separate tribal state, began agitation.

They raided tree nurseries, destroyed saplings and forest buildings. About 25 people have been killed in regular clashes with the police so far but nothing has been resolved. Meanwhile the Jharkhand leaders continue to use the sal-teakwood issue to stir the fury of the tribals. Said A.K. Roy, a Marxist MP from Bihar: "Now sal means Jharkhand, saguwan (teak) means Bihar."

A Nazm

SHAMS FARIDI

The date trees
Are
Slowly
Aging.

The torrents of boiling milk
Erupt even now
From the breasts
Of sandy lands.

The sad cycle of endless treasures
Long buried
In the chest of mountains
Will cease.

The camelcades
Lost in the sandy deserts
Will return
Soon.

Translated from the Urdu by K.K. Khullar

God: Two Moods

CHANDRAKANT KHOT

I

Where were you when breezes burnt?
Where were you when Surangi was widowed?
When Gurudutt broke, where were you?
When on the house of the mimosa indica
365 rocks fell, where were you?
When hell was rising in the wound of Ashwathama
Where were you?
Where were you?
Where were you?

     . . . .   Where must you be?
You denied your existence;
With Vishwamitra's hands
You threw away your existence;
By being an atheist . . . . Yourself.

II

I saw
Milk rushing to your existence
When I saw the breasts of your grace on shevaga tree
I caught you in my fingers, but you slipped away
With the feet of a bug; formless
You were without dress
At the time of my first coitus
You came with the blessings of rice akshata
In my son's marriage
You were the pyre on the day of death
When my girl-friend who was born blind
Began to recognize me by my breath . . . .
Were you in her eyes?
Unseen.

Translated from the Marathi by Prabhakar Machwe

Flood
(vellam)

VALLIKANNAN

Fresh floods in the river—
waves rising, ripples spreading froth and foam,
floods surging with froth and foam,
Whirling, curling, rolling
rushing waters running fast.
Why this haste, what to achieve?
All the floods are lost in the sea.

On the pavements in the cities
floods of humanity.
How many people, how many kinds!
Each within himself
lost in his own thought,
frenetic eddies in a macrocosm of machines.
Moving, walking, hurrying,
agitated throngs of shadows;
as today tomorrow,
today like yesterday.
Why this haste, what to achieve?
Life too is a flood;
is death the sea?

Translated from the Tamil by P.S. Sundararajan

Jealousy

RAFEEQUE RAAZ

It often so happens —
The stray dogs of the locality
Meet by the side of the drain
Drooping their heads, pondering over things unknown.
The shadow of my house
Becomes apprehensive of their sinister designs;
The street lamp lends color to their innocent thoughts.
And every fibre of my existence,

Withholding its breath, waits and wishes;
A beggar, a thief, turning up
And once again plundering the neighborhood
The pack of dogs, smelling the intruder, barking in chorus;
The nocturnal silence being torn into shreds,
And street after street walking aloud in shouting,
The bolted windows and barred shutters flying open
Every bed being forsaken;
And in the meantime
The sweet and lovable warmth of the forsaken bedrooms,
Turning into loveless chill.

Translated from the Kashmiri by A. M. Lone

Miss Tanuja Is All Tenderness

SUKHPAL VIR SINGH HASRAT

Miss Tanuja is all tenderness
She loves the animals even
No less than men.

With a smile on her lips
She feeds her dog with cakes
And lulls it to sleep
In her own bed.

If she find a child in tatters,
Getting down from her limousine,
With eyes full of tears
She slips a silver in his hand
And feels relieved.

Embracing her boy friend
Heaving a cold sigh
Remarks
"Honey, look what a poor little thing."

Translated from the Punjabi by Pritam Singh

Two Poems

DIVIK RAMESH

Feather

The door is left
open.

This beautiful feather would have
Glided through
that door.

The windows are closed—all.

Has a new bird arrived
On the tree in front?
                 Perhaps.
Or roosting there —
                 For long?

Ah! It is not always
Dust and storms
That enter through
The open door.

Sometimes it may be
A little feather too!

Bird's Wedding

For bird
There's no bridegroom's party.

For bird
There's no going to strange family.

For bird
There's no dowry.

The bird doesn't blush.

Yet, the bird gets married.
And it rains.

It rains, yet
No fancy clothes for
The bird.

The bird
　　　　flies
　　　　naked.
　　　　Naked
　　　　flies
The bird.
The bird
Doesn't commit
Suicide.

Translated from the Hindi by Arun Sedwal

A Lesson

K. S. NISAR AHMED

The poets of the Wordsworthian clan
counselled the beatnik Gregory Corso:
"Brother, open your inward eye and write,
Stop being a slave to the so-called reality
of life's misery and complexity.

Let a scene from nature
teach you a lesson.
Look at that tree, free from life's ugliness,
generous and harmless.
Be happy and give it your thanks."

Corso banged the table before him and said,
"This is the gratitude we have shown
to that noble, wonderful tree."

Translated from the Kannada by S. K. Desai

Snail

Jyotirmoy Datta

The snail
Does not appear to be a creation of nature.
Examine it closely:
It was born
In the strange imagination of a clever engineer
Like Leonardo da Vinci
Who decorated his life with rows of armored cars.

The whole snail is meant to outwit
An imagined enemy:
Eyes concealed on the front of its snout,
To be rolled back into the shell, if attacked,
Nose nowhere near the eyes or mouth,
Nostrils tucked under his waist —
If the hips of a snail can be called waist.

Though the snail is my neighbor
It is difficult to believe
He is a creature of this planet.
When I see the fort-like snail,
The whale steals my mind.

Thousands of miles away from us,
The whale roams about, lonely
Often reclining on her huge belly
Feeding babies with the milk of her breasts.
Compared with the snail
The whale's shape is much tidier.
We can imagine a loving whale.
Thinking of the impenetrable snail,
We feel related to the whale.

Translated from the Bengali by Prithvindra Chakravarti
with Ulli Beier

Aquarium

VIJAY DEV NARAIN SAHI

I invite you
to that imagined window
and to touch with your lips
the cold glass wall.
It will make you as pure as
the air atop a hill.

Across the window
you will find
two round and deep eyes—
like the sky itself
constantly regarding you.
As you grope your way
up the wall
those eyes will follow you.

Now you go back.
With your eyes downcast
ponder over the tender flowers,
white shells and ever green leaves
blossoming in this closet.

Let there be no anxiety
for those two eyes
if you care to look at them
again would gaze at you
without a blink
and whenever you will
you can slowly
walk up to the cold glass wall
and settle there against it
thirstless
pure.

Translated from the Hindi by Ajit Khullar

Friends

SARATKUMAR MUKHOPADHYAY

Get up in the morning
To hear he is dead,
With this hope I go to sleep every night.

I dream, someone like me
Carries his corpse,
Speaks at his funeral;

But the man does not die.
He stays stuck to me all day,
Barks, bites,
Prays for my death instead.

So you see how the nectar of mutual hatred
Helps us to live,
But determined
Not to let each other live in peace.

Translated from the Bengali by the author

The Masseuse

MALATHI RAO

Swatantra came running out of the house. But that signified nothing. For she always ran instead of walked. Time was very precious for Swatantra. "Not to pursue her own pleasures, mind you" — I argued myself blue in the face on this point, but my friends, Pushpa and Mrs. Saxena, insisted on disagreeing with me there. They judged Swatantra and condemned her. Pushpa and Mrs. Saxena behaved with that characteristic middle-class morality, confronted with a woman like Swatantra, who though poor bubbled with enviable vivacity and *joie de vivre*. Even with a hundred births neither of my two friends would have been anything but the birds of doom that they were. Well, as I was saying, Swatantra ran in order to get through her daily round as masseuse in half a dozen *kothis* of the *mohalla*. People were too used to seeing her slight form sprinting or walking very fast, the cloth bag clutched in her hand.

Seeing her thus erupt from behind the greenery of the Gupta house, I naturally made inquiries about her affairs. She called me "sister" for the simple reason that I had employed her as cook for two months last winter. Now she no longer cooked for me, but we had kept up the contact. Today, as usual, I asked her about her present activities.

"I went to Idgah," she told me, "to meet relatives."

"Oh."

"Also to inquire about an eligible boy . . . "

"Eligible boy? For whom?" I became curious.

"My daughter Baby . . . "

"That fourteen-year-old child?" I scolded Swatantra.

She clarified with a smile that was most disarming, "Not
fourteen . . . but going on seventeen, sister." I remembered it
was this smile, now lingering on in Swatantra's eyes in a rather
tantalizing manner, that had driven Pushpa and Mrs. Saxena
to pronounce their social and moral strictures on poor Swatantra.
She interrupted my thoughts, however, "You will come for
Baby's wedding, I hope? If this young man agrees, the marriage
will be in August."

"August isn't very far . . . " I said.

"Yes, and there'll be a hundred preparations to think of
and to make before the wedding. My husband is no good at
these things." All the same, Swatantra continued to smile as
though she had no worry in the world. Perhaps she will receive
all the help that she needs from the Sethjis she works for, I
thought. Swatantra's husband had remained a nonentity ever
since I had known her.

"The boy . . . what does he do?" I asked.

"He is O.K. By the way, he was not home yesterday."

"You are not giving Baby also to agriculture, are you? Like
your first daughter."

"This boy," said Swatantra, "works in a grain shop. He writes
accounts. No, not the fields again. One is enough." Then, as an
afterthought, she asked me, "Is anyone cooking for you at
present?"

"No."

"I'm free in the evenings, sister, and I can come . . . You
know how sorry I was to leave you . . . last February."

"No . . . It won't work . . . "

"I still don't know why you threw me out . . . but all the
same . . . you are my 'sister' and nothing can come between us
. . . " she said and gave me that warm smile again. Of course,
she made me feel quite a heel for the suspicions I'd entertained
about her. Looking at Swatantra, I felt my own part in the whole
business had not been very gracious. However, she was in a
hurry and time was very precious for Swatantra. I saw her now
wiggle away to Sethji Gheewalla's house where she gave an oil
massage to the first daughter-in-law, every afternoon of the week.

I stood for a moment, wondering if I'd ever know the truth about Swatantra. Come on, I scolded myself, as I resumed my walk . . . after all, how much did I care for her . . . what was my commitment to her . . . how was I in any way better than Pushpa or Mrs. Saxena . . . or that class of women for whom people like Swatantra were merely like the furniture one used and discarded.

I couldn't tell you with any exactitude . . . this or that was my grievance against Swatantra. I was happy enough with her until my two friends, Pushpa and Mrs. Saxena, came to visit me one afternoon. It was winter and we sat on the terrace. The talk turned to the difficulty of finding good servants and I told them about my new cook, Swatantra. "Only she is not just a cook. She is a masseuse as well," I said laughing.

"How?"

"Well, she goes to a number of houses in the *mohalla* and gives the overweight Sethjis oil massage, ordinary massage and so on. Three rupees per massage, she charges."

"And when does she cook for you?" Mrs. Saxena asked.

"In the evenings. Exactly at six p.m. she is climbing my staircase . . . and she is through with the cooking within an hour. That's one thing about her . . . she races helter-skelter . . . "

Mrs. Saxena had looked askance at me. "To my mind, some-how all this doesn't seem right, Anandi . . . Cook and masseuse don't go together, you know."

"Think of the aesthetic aspect of it," butted in Pushpa. "She goes and kneads all those fleshy bodies . . . and then she comes and with those very hands she kneads your dough . . . chhee . . . chhee . . . chhee . . . !"

Put that way, it did sound obscene. I had visions of mounds of flesh in the nude and the small ball of dough in my kitchen and I felt depressed about the whole thing.

"What you can do," suggested Mrs. Saxena, "is to ask her to wash her hands with Carbolic soap before she puts her hands to your pots and pans."

Swatantra, of course, never bothered to wash her hands if I didn't happen to be in the kitchen. Sometimes I stood there until she had scrubbed her hands. With a ready smile she com-

plied, but the next day she'd forget again or was too lazy to do
it. I began to think this slovenliness was a part of her whole
personality. Most evenings I had to clear up the mess in the
kitchen, after she'd left. What I discovered was a total lack of
discipline and professionalism in her. She really was no cook. I
was sure she was not so bad a masseuse. After all, what skill did
it require to pound at extra rolls of flesh on the Sethjis, young
and old.

"A rolling pin flattens out any paunch in one week,"
Swatantra said with a laugh, as she rolled out chapatis in my
kitchen.

"A rolling pin?"

"Yes, sister, a rolling pin. I use it on some of the ladies . . .
I just roll off their extra flesh as I roll off this chapati . . . "

"You look so thin yourself," I said, "where do you get the
strength to flatten out the fat accumulated over the years through
pure ghee and laziness?"

"Want a demonstration?" Her silver earrings twinkled as
she turned round to me, with a smile.

"Oh no, no . . . thank you." It was enough that she was cooking for me. I had no intention of hiring her services as masseuse
as well. There I'd draw the line—where making use of another
person's skill was concerned. She'd knead me and pound me as
she did my chapati dough. Perhaps use a rolling pin on me too.
Not that I'm like one of those fat Sethjis. Scratch me and tickle.
She'd roll me this way and that. Go over every inch of my body.
Some said, it toned up your muscles, took years off you, gave you
a new feeling altogether. Bearer of the new elixir of life,
Swatantra was very much in demand in the *mohalla*. But I drew
the line. In fact, I had a mania about this business of touching. I
lived alone and touch was something totally absent in my life.
I wanted no masseuse now, even if she held out the promise
of toned-up muscles and dreams of renewed youth.

I needed a cook however and Swatantra was a god-send to
me. I had found her at a time when I had given up all hope of
ever finding help and I intended keeping her. The only fly in
the ointment was that she pursued this other profession as well
. . . that of a masseuse. The timings did not clash, no. But it

created distrust and suspicion in me about her sense of cleanliness. I was often forced to spy on her. One evening I caught
her. She was pounding away at the dough, her hands all floury. She
didn't bat an eyelid. "I'll wash them now," she said with a laugh
and a wiggle of her shapely bottom.

"Now? After I've told you a hundred times to wash your
hands as soon as you step into the kitchen!"

That evening I was upset. I saw Mrs. Saxena's point. Cook
and masseuse didn't go together. I thought I must correct this
anomalous situation. I decided I'd tell Swatantra I didn't want
her any more. But the next evening . . . she came with her
nine-year-old son all muffled up in a shawl and she made him
sit on a foot-stool in the corner of the kitchen. I didn't have the
heart to tell her anything.

During this time, Mrs. Saxena took to visiting me any time
of the day. Somehow the conversation always turned to Swatantra,
after a few minutes. Her prurience irritated me. When she came
alone, that is without Pushpa, I found her easier to handle. But
with each of her visits I realized my own vulnerability, my
"Achilles' heel." Mrs. Saxena always had something nasty to say
about Swatantra, and she knew this is where she had me in her
clutches. I always made a desperate attempt to defend my
companion-cum-cook-cum-"sister." On one occasion I happened
to say, "She hardly looks a cook, when she makes up her face
. . . and dresses up . . . "

"What! She uses make-up, your cook?" Mrs. Saxena raised
her eyebrows.

I began hotly, "Sitaji, just because Swatantra is poor . . . "

But Mrs. Saxena was tittering, "You better investigate a
little deeper into this masseuse business, Anandi."

"Why?"

"Well, don't mistake me. She might be having a bit of fun,
you know. You never can tell what goes on in these big houses
under the guise of masseuse and all that nonsense."

"Who would be interested in her, Sitaji?" I asked.

"Who, she asks! Why, the Sethjis themselves . . . believe me."

I pondered for a moment over what Mrs. Saxena had said.
How could I believe her, for what she was saying was mere con-
jecture.

"All that I can say is . . . the poor creature is putting all her strength into rolling away the extra weight of the Sethjis with a rolling pin, and the fat old ladies dream of becoming young and beautiful!"

"What rolling pin?"

"Why, the ordinary one," I said.

She laughed loudly as though it were a big joke — as indeed it was. "Your Swatantra . . . !" she chortled, shaking her head. After a time she left, quite unconvinced about the rolling pin.

I was determined not to be browbeaten by either Pushpa or Mrs. Saxena. The following Saturday, they came face to face with Swatantra in my house. At least they had the good sense not to stare at her, though it was the first time they were setting eyes on her. However, my two friends didn't fail to exchange looks. "Namasteji," Swatantra said with a smile to my guests. "Come and eat; dinner is ready." Her smile to me seemed like a silver lining in the dark mentality of my friends.

Swatantra served us hot chapatis, vegetables and coconut chutney. We moved to the living room after dinner. Swatantra had left, but her presence lingered.

"There is something in her eyes," said Pushpa, moving her own eyes like a cheap actress.

"She has very pretty eyes . . . " I said.

"And her smile . . . " added Mrs. Saxena, with sour disapproval. "She is the kind of woman I wouldn't admit into my house for a minute." She gave a mock shudder.

"Why?" I asked.

Mrs. Saxena shook her head as though she didn't want to say anything further.

"Why?"

Pushpa said, "You know why."

"Tell me, why are you both against her?"

However, I was astonished by Mrs. Saxena's lightness of tone as she said, "Masseuse, cook . . . whatever it be, Anandi . . . her main object seems to be to please men. She is far too attractive . . . "

"She pleases me . . . and I'm not." A man, I wanted to say.

"You are a simpleton," cut in Mrs. Saxena, rudely.

"No," I protested. "I don't think you are right to judge by appearances. Just because Swatantra is poor, you think she has no right to be attractive."

"There is no mistaking the type." Mrs. Saxena's own type was that of the beard-and-moustache-growing female. She also had the hard tough body of a prize-fighter. "That petite body would serve as a pretty morsel to any Sethji or his son . . . or sons."

Pushpa gave a whoop of laughter, while I muttered under my breath: "It is plain jealousy, to talk of things about which we know nothing . . . "

"At times the fat Sethji might be playing the pimp . . . to keep the husband happy and not to allow him to stray far," Mrs. Saxena observed.

Well, enough was enough, I thought. They had gone too far. I had seen their dirty minds. It was clear I must defend Swatantra from my friends. But before I could say what I wanted to, Mrs. Saxena once again broke out. "What I really wanted to say, Anandi, was that she goes from house to house, touches bodies, limbs, backs and God knows what else, of all kinds of people . . . : well, only women, she says . . . but who knows . . . how do you know what to believe and what not to believe, and then she comes and touches your food . . . now don't you think, she might be a carrier of all kinds of diseases . . . I don't know, perhaps not of cancer but all the other contagious diseases . . . "

I spluttered, wheezed, lost my voice, found it . . . all in one split second. My friends, I wondered if I should still call them that, had declared open battle with Swatantra, whom they had marked as their prey, from the moment they had heard about her. Their high-powered missiles threatened to win the day. I said in a small voice, "She is a poor woman . . . merely trying to make ends meet . . . "

But they turned the screws pretty well into Swatantra's coffin before they left. If I had any qualms about giving her the marching papers, my friends very kindly offered to do it for me.

"Of a very different sort. Not like you or me . . . " said Mrs. Saxena.

"Just to say it in one word," added Pushpa, "it is the class she belongs to. When have the lower classes had any morals?"

"Of course, she is not educated," I said, making a last-ditch effort to save Swatantra from the injustice of her "sisters," from her middle-class judges. I had truly come to like Swatantra, with her warm smile, her prattle about her daughter married to an agriculturist in Sonepet, and Baby who was fourteen last year, but seventeen today.

One evening in the last week of February, Swatantra had come early and said, "You are going to Nandnagri with me."

"What for?"

"You'll visit my home. There is only one room . . . of course . . . "

"Don't you eat?" I teased her. "Where d'you cook?"

"I cook in one corner of the room, sister."

"And the bathroom?"

"One has to bathe outside in the summer," she said. "In winter you manage somehow. As for the latrine, Baby and I are put to the most terrible inconvenience day after day, as we have to use the common latrines . . . some half a furlong away. It's awful . . . "

I thought she was very upset by the whole thing but she smiled readily enough when I said, "I'd like to see where you live . . . but not today."

"I know you'll never come."

"Of course I will. I'll come for Baby's wedding."

And it seemed now I'd attend Baby's wedding, if that fellow at the grain shop said "yes." Though things were really not the same . . . At least, I could not see Swatantra as I knew her first. Or even perhaps as she really was. Who knows which was the real Swatantra? But the Swatantra that I now saw was the one Mrs. Saxena and Pushpa had conjured up for me. Whenever I saw her on the road and she smiled at me, I wondered . . . which Sethji is she carrying on with? Or could she be carrying on with half a dozen of them at the same time? Such was the power Mrs. Saxena had wielded over me. It seemed Swatantra was totally unaware of what went on in my mind. Otherwise how else do you explain her wanting me to attend Baby's wedding?

A word about the manner in which she had to leave my service. Well, as I said, my friends had finally worn me down with their missiles against Swatantra. And one evening, it was exactly two months to the day since she'd entered my service, I told her I wouldn't need her any more. She joked and laughed and asked me why. I told her the doctor had advised me not to eat chapatis.

"Who is that foolish doctor?" she said. "In fact, you *must* eat chapatis."

After a great deal of banter in a similar vein, finally I convinced her that I wouldn't die of starvation sans her cooking. Even so the poor thing brought me food, in a brass tiffin carrier, for two days following her dismissal. I wolfed down the food shamelessly.

Of course, once broken, things can never be the same. Mrs. Saxena and Pushpa have gone out of my life. It came as a reaction after this Swatantra business. Truly, they had no business to butt in as they did. As I told you, Swatantra and I keep up a sort of contact. I see her running from house to house, always in a hurry. A masseuse in great demand.

Seven Poems

JOHN TAGLIABUE

Insistent Hindu and otherwise

The joys of sex are so saucy so sumptuous
    so both tangible and intangible
    so raucous though often quiet
    so undescribable yet alert
    so cool and in fire and
    renewing, so concerned
with grasping yet ungraspable, so in our possession like
    our memories or stagings of the gods
    yet a form of non-possessive love
so unique and multiplying that tigers and gazelles are born from
    their shadows and murmurings
so subtle and cosmic and necessary that clouds and downpours
    and rivers are synonymous with them
    and amorous motion.

A pantheistic painter of signs

He climbed upon the billboard like a monkey or like a
    god who was to
surprise himself and with his paint brush made letters of
    all colors and as he
was swashbuckling and as he whistled as he shook his head
    in obeisance to the planetary motions
and molecular messages the letters that he depicted grew
    taller and taller, they led an
almost independent life and he and the letters and this
    gave him enough energy to stand
on top of a flying letter and invent another language,
    this in turn predicted more
    epics, love lyrics, and
descriptions of all kinds. Some of the billboards, monkeys and
    gods disappeared but the spirit of
    literature was vital.

You can go very far at that

The 1st time I learned to spell elephant I was transported,
    the elephant thanked me,
I rode on him until I could spell India and Hindu and
    "do you love me?"
again the elephant answered yes and this time with a
    chorus of tigers,
soon I was able to spell Blake and forests and the world
    increased in wonder,
I didn't want to stop riding, it was great to be up there
    and I was really dressed up
and there were festivals in every village that I entered.
    When I opened a book birds flew out
    or rabbits came out of a word.
Then I saw a procession of elephants and even the Buddha.

Om and Shanti

Riding a Hindu horse one went all over
    the Cosmos
it never stopped becoming as colorful as
    It Is
other people felt free to ride on this horse
    as all people and plants
and animals and planets felt free all
    the time and Eternity
to babble about God. I slept by the
    dream of Shiva
I awoke by the Dance of Karma. We
    all saw the Horse
feeding and sporting in the Cosmos and never
    can the languages of God
cease to be colorful since we were Singing
    on the Horse.

Where to, O unknown Soul,
O unknown Universe?

It, he, she, they, covered with a bright gold cloth,
it, the unknown dead body, was carried with light gold
as they ran soon after dawn, running, carrying
it, he, she, they, on a litter, it was as if there was already
a fire, running fast to the cremation ground and Ganga;
the unknown body was as light as the breath of
    a living person.

Benares

A dime a dozen —
more like a rupee
a thousand — any
way many most
millions by the Ganges,
young boys, thin, dark,
large eyes, smiling, waiting
to make a sell, offer for
a rupee or two all those
scented prayer necklaces,
the huge Sun is rising at
this very moment as
tourists in a daze buy
a dozen, as thousands
from all over India
or the Hindu world respond
actively respond with some
sort of yoga some sort of
hope to the wide river
and the expansive light.

Bhumisparshamudra

I touch the ground
meaning I've been here before,
every plant has preached my
enlightenment.

House of a thousand doors

MEENA ALEXANDER

This house has a thousand doors
the sills are cut in bronze
three feet high
to keep out snakes,
toads, water rats
that shimmer in the bald reeds
at twilight
as the sun burns down to the Kerala coast.

The roof is tiled in red
pitched with a silver lightning rod,
a prow, set out from land's end
bound nowhere.
In dreams
waves lilt, a silken fan
in grandmother's hands
shell colored, utterly bare
as the light takes her.

She kneels at each
of the thousand doors in turn
paying her dues.
Her debt is endless.
I hear the flute played in darkness,
a bride's music.
A poor forked thing,
I watch her kneel in all my lifetime
imploring the household gods
who will not let her in.

Woman

SIDDALINGA PATTANASHETTI

Woman
is a problem negative:
print it,
enlarge it, do what you will,
as you rub the chemicals
of desire,
the picture, the same old picture,
gets clearer and clearer.

Translated from the Kannada by A. K. Ramanujan

A Prayer for Lisa & Harvey

JOHN REPP

I rub your wooden belly sometimes
when I write poems, Lord Buddha.
You remember, Lisa gave you
to me when there were no poems.
She dragged me to meet Harvey,
who played wicked slide guitar,
who drove us nuts chanting *Ram Ram Hari Ram* all the way
to Maine & cried for a lost mandala.

Keep them
themselves, Lord Buddha.
Keep Harvey chanting the blues
with wide, liquid eyes.
Keep Lisa as I see her
in dream sometimes, in long skirts twirling,
flinging Buddhas everywhere.

Woman On The Beach

KERSY D. KATRAK

Coming around the bend we felt the head
Of subtly turning air, the changing sound
Of larger tides beating against the land.
Living beside the sea we sense them first:
The first small signs of cold that apprehend
Our short and sudden winter. As we came round
The last flat bend, my wife smiled gently. Brandy, I said:
Courvoisier Brandy. Winter became a thirst;
A singing in the ears, the senses sharp and free.
I whistled and changed gears as we went forth
To take the last steep drop that meets the sea:
Turning towards the house I felt the wind
Pointing its finger North.

Details sometimes intrude upon our lives and point
Towards the center. This woman was a detail
I saw her first
From out the corner of my eye
Behind the car, I braked and swerved
My wife clucking annoyance, and parked elsewhere.
There she lay
Flat on her back, her elbows propped her up:
Dressed shabbily but not a beggar.
From time to time she moved and scraped
A little backwards: dressed shabbily
But not a beggar . . .
Three hours later between the trifle
And brandy, I found the hard
Center of my vague unease.
I had seen such movements before
In puppies whipped to death, in mangled cats,
Men hit by trucks and crawling blind
Across the road to some imagined shelter:
I had seen those slow
Witless movements before: her back was broken.

I ran:
Obeying as we always do

Some law of more than necessary love
Always too late.
When I reached the front gate she was gone.
Taken away, I thought, strangers have helped
She could not have moved far unhelped . . .

Facing the winter stars
Suddenly bright,
Suddenly apprehensive for my wife alone
And sleeping, I turned upstairs and ran.
Counted my possessions and was relieved
To find them there. Counted my life
And found it limited but good.
Turning the sheets I slipped beside my wife,
Half asleep she understood
My need for reassurance and comforted my pride.
Before I slept I said a prayer for my wife
Having accounted all, but not accounted God
Who pauses to disrupt
With something much like love, the smallest life.

Next morning was the first cold day with hot
Winter breakfast on the plate.
I wore my three-piece suit, we talked and ate
Relieved at having found the usual things to say.
Turning towards the car I saw the crowd
Two hundred yards behind and walked that way
Knowing what I would find.

She lay there as I looked and mind
Outstripped its midweek calm:
This was Thursday. And that red horror there,
The back indeed was broken but there was more:
The flesh had torn, smashed, pulped, retreated, to expose
The hidden and interior bone.
That calm unnerving whiteness was untouched whilst
        in the red
Flies moved in swarms.
                    What madman
Demon husband, raging lover, or what claws
Of hell or powers of love had done this;

From what great heights dropped her
And left her at my doorstep to be found
By me, neglected, and from there to crawl
Blindly towards the mothering sea before she died:
I would not know.
                              But my reflex was instant:
Doors shut in my mind.
Wipe the mouth, adjust the tie:
Call the police I said
Fighting panic at my own
Disproportionate sense of loss:
Fighting to keep together
All that I knew: the house, the small
Patrimony of land, the lawn where winter flowers had
        grown.
But knew this once for all: the only flesh
With which one may identify
Death, is one's own.

Stars

SITANSHU YASHASCHANDRA

The astronomer-sage
who first imagined constellations
how frightened he must have felt
of stars scattered all over the universe;
I know.

Stars are really frightful.
          Or lovely.
Stars never set.
Eyes dimmed by the lustre of the sun
Can't see them, that's all.

Early morning
when stars start disappearing one after the other
only the broken shape of leaves
of the opposite *neem* tree-top
comes to the rescue of eyes.
Beauty when not frightful, can be so fragile.
That's the reason why at times
I wish to take my eyes out of their hollows
and place them on a mountain top
to see the beauty of stars from near them
—without a thought for my safety.
In these ugly lanes of the sun
I'll manage with a stout stick.
But
then
I remember my beloved's momentary face.
—I need my eyes.

Translated from the Gujarati by Varsha Das

On The Evaluation of
Creative Literature

Daya Krishna

Literature, like art, is an attempt to catch and articulate the significant moments of one's experience and, at a deeper level, to explore the depths and dark recesses of experience with the help of the symbol and, at a still deeper level, to detach, re-form and re-shape experience into an autonomous, self-sufficient, significant whole whose filiations to that from which it has been detached, though certainly there, are irrelevant in terms of significance. The symbol always goes beyond that which it symbolizes. It does not merely articulate but it explores and creates.

The symbol is the dividing line between the arts; their use, the dividing line between the arts and the sciences. Each type of symbol sets problems of its own—the problems of technique in the arts. Mere technique marks the craftsman. One who articulates, explores and creates is the artist.

Word—the written Word—is the symbol that marks out literature from the other arts. The strength and weakness of literature lie in words. The whole world of semantic reference is its bane and its delight. Its perennial use for indicative, persuasive and imperative purposes is the greatest temptation to which it is constantly exposed. Always in danger of slipping into the pedestrian uses of language, it has at its command, resources of such richness as none of the symbolic media used by the other arts can ever dream of.

Lingering over moments surcharged with significance, that is Memory. It is the primary art-form—the attempt to hold

what was significant, to circumvent the irreversible process of
Time, to clip its wings and freeze it into an ever-alive but immobile Present. But Memory is no mere memory. In circling
round the significant moment, in lovingly fondling the images
that arise, it subtly changes the contours of sense and feeling
and colors it in tints more appropriate to one's own sense of
significance and form. Imagination, thus, is never far from
Memory. In fact, it is already implicit in it. The so-called falsify-
ing function of Memory is its imaginative aspect which people
decry because of their excessive preoccupation with the veracity
aspect of it.

Image, common to both memory and imagination, is caught
by the symbol and given a fixity and depth which it did not
possess before. The image is too much in the present and too
much floating on the surface. The symbol gives it an anchorage
and a dimension and all that was submerged behind the image
is caught in the net and gradually revealed by the symbol. Striking deep into the past, it projects into the future also and,
thus, bends the straight line of time into a closed circle where
everything returns to itself and the whole is self-sufficient unto
itself.

The symbol touches experience at many points and many
levels. Experience, however, is too ambiguous a word and means
all sorts of things to all sorts of people. To many, the only
experience is sense-experience or, at least, experience in its
fullest sense, the paradigm for all other "experiences." But sensory
experience or any other experience is always "lived through,"
and that which is "lived through" is hardly understood either
in terms of concepts or meaning, significance and value. The
attempt to understand in terms of generalized, inter-related
concepts leads to science on the one hand and philosophy on
the other. The attempt to understand in terms of meaning,
significance and value leads, on the other hand, to art and religion in different directions. Concerned with these, the arts
and religions have meaning, significance and value in themselves while the conceptual constructions of science and philosophy are interesting only in so far as they help us in understanding the phenomena.

The development of experience beyond the sensory level is accomplished through the symbol. But the primary use of the symbol among men is not in the articulation, exploration or creation of new levels of experience but in a constant interchange of thought and emotion at the ordinary level, or for influencing the thoughts, feelings and actions of men in the desired directions. The artist treats and uses the symbols in a different way than either the scientist or the philosopher or the common man. They are intrinsically important for him as for none other and he uses them, at the deepest level, to detach experience from all the irrelevancy in which it is embedded and with which it is surrounded. The symbol is the living tool with which the artist creates a pure world of experienced significance. Art is not "the imitation of an imitation" as Plato thought. Rather it is the distilled essence of experience more alive than experience itself. The distillation, however, is not in terms of concepts where Plato thought essences to lie, but in terms of significance and value caught in the concrete image which may be considered as the feeling-counterpart of the conceptual universal.

The symbol, in the hands of the artist, does not *primarily* serve for purposes of communication as many have thought. Its function rather is to abstract, articulate, explore and create. Art, ultimately, can only be contemplated. Its contemplation can only lead to the re-living of another's experience, the becoming aware of shades, nuances and aspects one had never suspected in one's experience before, the participation in experience before, the participation in experiences one had never known. Art dissociates feeling from desire, emotion from impulse, sentiment from action. Its measure of failure is its failure in effecting this dissociation, so difficult to achieve. The perversion of art is the other way round: to influence feelings to arouse desire, to enflame emotions to arouse impulse, to strengthen sentiment to arouse to action.

The perversion is not felt as a perversion by many who seek sensation or instruction or moral elevation or religious exaltation or political passion. These, and many besides these, are worthy ends of human action. But the person obsessed with a

single value tends to treat all others as instrumental to its reali-
zation. This, though an understandable weakness, is funda-
mentally wrong; for values have an autonomy which is realized
only by those who pursue them. The integration of values which
are intrinsic and autonomous cannot be achieved, as many
seem to think, by the hierachic subordination of some to some
other. It can only be achieved by an acceptance of their autonomy and equal validity at the personal and social levels
simultaneously. Each has to be understood in its own terms and
not in those of any other.

This simple and obvious truth has been profoundly mis-
interpreted in the slogan "Art for Art's sake." As a protest
against the perversion of art, it is amply justified. As a recall to the immanent, autonomous values in terms of which
alone any work of art can be relevantly judged, it is perfectly
all right. But as suggesting that art has got nothing to do with
world or life or experience, it is supremely mistaken. Art is an
approach to world, life and experience co-ordinate with other
approaches. It can neither supplant them nor be a substitute for
them. But neither can they, singly or collectively, be a substitute
for it. Science and Philosophy, Art and Religion provide approaches that cannot be exchanged for one another. Art is no
ivory-tower; but neither is science nor philosophy nor religion,
though many seem to think so. But science or philosophy or religion is not social reform or moral pursuit or the production of
utility-goods. But neither is art any such thing, though many
well-meaning people want otherwise. And didn't somebody say
that the way to some nasty place is paved with good intentions?

Words are tricky tools, too much loaded in one direction.
They declare, cajole, persuade, command, interject, express,
arouse. To turn them to the use of art is to bend them against
their inclination, to make them forget their function. Or, to
make their normal function serve unwittingly something else,
something deeper, something different. The story of literature,
like that of man, is the story of the Temptation, the Fall, and
the occasional Resurrection. Not so occasional as in the realm
of the spirit, still it is not as frequent as many imagine. The
subtle transformation of Temptation into the lure for horizons,

of the Fall into the thrust down into the deep of the roots for the sap to turn to the skies and beyond is the secret alchemy both of life and art.

Word is the most pervading symbol man has created. It touches experience at all points and penetrates at all levels. The feeling that glides softly like a breeze, the passion that rages like a storm, the ambition that stings into feverish days and sleepless nights, the dull, drowsy-heavy-laden boredom that settles like a stupor on the heart and turns everything into a dusty haze with sand-particles crinkling under one's tongue, the daily round of a dozen cares, the Moment that leaps across and spans the horizons, the quiet strength of the mountains, the stately grace of trees that stretch their arms to the loving wind, the losing depth of the seas, the resplendent light of the sun, the gladdening madness of the moon—all these and a million other things that move the human heart and the human mind to song and tears and laughter and aspiration, it touches and penetrates and envelops and illumines.

The conflict between one good and another good and the awareness of something beyond all goods permeates the human situation. The private and the public good, the good which is neither private nor public and the good which is no good but rather a state of being, haunt perennially the human mind. Action always *seeks* a value and through seeking gives unity, meaning and significance to time in which our life is inextricably involved. Contemplation does not *seek*; it only contemplates and, thus, stills time. Between action and contemplation, art inclines to the latter though the natural inclination of the word is in the direction of the former. The dialectic between time and the timeless is the essence of human experience. The action-oriented person treats the contemplative as an escapist dweller in some cloud-cuckoo land. The contemplative just contemplates the sweeping beauty of motion and immortalizes it in some cosmic dance of Shiva. But the man of action does not dance. Rather, he is the Absolute on the white charger whose beauty can be seen only by the eye of the artist which contemplates it. Gross is the field of action; the subtle escapes it. External are the ends of action; an inner transformation of consciousness, the ultimate goal of contemplation.

The continuous transformation of the temporal into the time-less is the essence of art. But the temporal is many-faceted and multi-dimensional. The stream that flows as conscious experience has depths unrevealed on the surface. Art not only makes us aware of those depths but makes us *hold* them in the clear light of consciousness. The stream not only has depth but flows on towards the sea, to become the ocean it aspires to be. This ocean, art attempts to embody and sometimes comes miraculously close to it. Of the arts, literature is perhaps the one that attempts this most often and in its greatest creations comes close to realizing what experience is always trying to be.

The truth of experience is the only truth that art or, for that matter, life knows. Science and philosophy seek truth in terms of theoretic coherence; art and religion in terms of realized experience. The poet's moon does not exist in the scientist's world and the moon which the scientist knows is irrelevant to the poet's world. The love that makes the heart beat and the world glow with a suffused wonder is unknown and irrelevant to the physiologist, psychologist and sociologist who try to grasp it in their different ways. But, equally, what they say is irrelevant to the lover as he lives through and feels his experience. Love, in this, is akin to art and religion. Like them, it uses memory and imagination to create a world of experienced significance which has little relation to the world as explored, articulated and understood by science and philosophy. Unlike art, however, it is never, even potentially, a publicly shared experience. Unlike religion, on the other hand, it is never the affair of a solitary which religion ultimately and essentially is. A semi-conscious creation between two persons, the others are irrelevant to it. They may help or hinder or be indifferent but, in no case, may they be invited to participate in it. Their participation is an intrusion that breaks the charmed circle and if the participation be helped by one of the lovers himself it gives rise to what is known as jealousy.

Science creates the elements through nuclear fission and the compounds through synthesis in the laboratory and the factory. Art parallels this in the world of experienced significance through what may be called symbolic dissociation and symbolic synthesis. The former disintegrates the feelings associated with the familiar symbols; the latter recombines the familiar into a novel pattern. Both are present to some degree in every work of art, but the emphasis is always varied and different.

Art, as we have already said, is concerned with human experience in terms of its experienced significance. Literature as an art form is, however, primarily concerned with experience as an interaction between persons. The feeling for Nature has inspired some great poetry, but landscape-painting catches it even better. On the other hand, even the greatest portraits of Rembrandt epitomizing the experience of a life-time seem inadequate as a medium when compared with what literature can do in the field. The greatest triumph of dramatic illustration in stone and paint seem to fall short of the achievements in the field of literature concerning the same themes. The triumphs are, in fact, of a different order and in a different direction.

The interactive experience between persons is the central theme of human life as lived and literature celebrates this to the utmost extent. Love, jealousy, ambition, rage, hatred, lust, sympathy, tenderness, sorrow—the whole gamut of emotions between persons is its joy and its delight. The curve of the emotions is its curve; their dynamic, its dynamic. The drama that goes on between persons daily is its theme; their anguish, its anguish; their ecstasy, its ecstasy.

Moral values pervade this realm, the realm of inter-personal interaction. It is thus that all great literature centers around moral conflict. The essence, however, lies not in morality but in conflict. Literature does not moralize; it only illuminates the moral conflict. The saint who has never been tempted hardly interests the literary artist. The Buddha seated in deep meditation may challenge the chisel of the sculptor or the brush of the painter, but never the pen of the writer. The man who is tempted but does not succumb to the tempation interests the writer only a little. It is the one who falls and yet, in falling, redoubles his grandeur that fascinates the literary artist. Or, subtler still, falling externally one who achieves internal redemption, or falling internally, one who achieves external success fascinates him still more.

Literature, to the moralist, therefore, almost always appears immoral. It is not partial to good as the moralist would like it to be. Rather, it is fascinated by evil and wants to explore its innermost processes and understand how it overcomes and is overcome by good. To the living man, however, it is the most fascinating of all the arts as it alone gives him an insight into his life as lived and experienced and, in the process, takes him beyond the conflict of good and evil.

Politics, in the strict sense, has never concerned literature. The business of government is mostly left alone by it. Only as drama does it ever concern itself with it. The kings and their battles or loves or adventures have all been written about in the past. More recently, the betrayal of values, the subtle intertwining of good and evil, has been its theme. Masses in revolt, the struggle against injustice, the wars and revolutions— whatever is written about, the theme is always the drama in the minds of men or the drama outside them or the subtle intertwining of the two that is dealt with.

Literature as an art-form, thus, serves neither morals nor politics nor truth as sought in philosophy or science. In its evaluation as a creative art form, therefore, they are utterly irrelevant. But in providing a background understanding for critical evaluation of some types of creative literature, they are indispensable as an informational framework without which the first steps in intuiting the sense cannot be undertaken. This is particularly true of those literary works which presuppose a philosophic-cum-religious background or which ostensibly concern themselves with socio-political issues that agitate their own times. With morals, on the other hand, what is required is a deep lived experience of the values that agitate one being and pull it in different directions.

These, however, are only the prerequisites of the task of critical evaluation of creative literature. They do not provide the criteria in terms of which it is to be judged. These can only be found in the intensive depth, the extensive comprehensiveness, the creative novelty with which the lived experience is articulated, explored and created in the literary work that is to be evaluated and judged: any other criteria will either be purely technical or extrinsic to the work and, thus, be irrelevant.

Notes on Contributors

AGYEYA (S. H. VATSYAYAN, b. 1911), a leading Hindi poet and novelist, won the 1979 Bhartiya Jnanpith Award * K. S. NISAR AHMED (b. 1936) has published many volumes of poetry in Kannada * MEENA ALEXANDER (b. 1951), whose volume of poetry is *Stone Roots*, was born in Allahabad and teaches at Fordham U., N.Y. * U. R. ANANTHAMURTHY, author of the well-known novel, *Samskara*, is Professor of English at the U. of Mysore * ASHOKAMITRAN (J. THYAGARAJAN, b. 1931) has established himself as a leading short story writer in Tamil. He lives in Madras and edits a Tamil small magazine * GHANSHYAM ASTHANA, a poet and painter, teaches English at Agra College * MANOHAR BANDHYOPADHYAY has translated the well-known Hindi epic, *Kamayanii*, into English * VASANT BAPAT (b. 1922) teaches Sanskrit at R.R. College, Bombay * SHIV KUMAR BATALVI (1937-73) has won many honors and awards for his collections of poetry * V. G. BHAT (b. 1923) works for the government and resides in Bombay * J. BIRJE-PATIL is Professor of English at M.S. U. of Baroda. He produces plays and is author of books on Shakespeare and T.S. Eliot * PRITHVINDRA CHAKRAVARTY (b. 1933) studied at Santiniketan and the U. of Chicago and now teaches at the U. of Papua and New Guinea * G. S. SHARAT CHANDRA lives in Tallahassee, Florida, and has published collections of poetry in the U.S. and England * BIRENDRA CHATTOPADHYAY (b. 1920) was considered an important Bengali poet of social consciousness during the 1940s * RAJ CHENGAPPA is a journalist for the popular weekly, *India Today* (a *Time* magazine look-alike); his article in this edition is presented courtesy of *India Today* * DEVDAS CHHOTRAY (b. 1946) will soon be publishing his first volume of verse. He is in the Indian Administrative Service * DILIP CHITRE (b. 1938) lives in Bombay; he has published award-winning poetry and fiction in Marathi, and his book of poems in English, *Travelling In A Cage*, was published by Clearing House, Bombay * TONY CONNOR, British by birth, is Professor of Literature at Wesleyan U. and author of five volumes of poetry. He spent four months in India in 1980 * KEKI N. DARUWALLA, a senior police executive, has published both poetry and fiction in English * ASHOK DAS's poems included here are his first published ones * JAGANNATH PRASAD DAS (b. 1936) is in the Indian Administrative Service, posted in Delhi. He has published poetry in Oriya and English, and his paintings have been exhibited around the country * KAMALA DAS, who writes in both Malalayam and English and is author of several books, resides in Bombay * SISIR KUMAR DAS (b. 1936) is Tagore Professor of Bengali, Delhi U. * VARSHA DAS works for the Directorate of Adult Education, New Delhi, and has translated many poems into English * JYOTIRMOY DATTA (b. 1936) edited *Kolkata*, a literary magazine that was banned under the Emergency; he is now a freelance journalist in Calcutta * S. K. DESAI, well-known Kannada novelist, is Professor of English at Shivaji U., Kohlapur * EUNICE DE SOUZA, whose poems explore the Goan-Catholic milieu, teaches at St. Xavier's College, Bombay * DHOOMIL (SUDAMA PRASAD, 1943-75) lived most of his life in Varanasi * NISSIM EZEKIEL, the leading Indo-English poet, teaches English and American Literature at the U. of Bombay * RUTH FAINLIGHT lives in London, England, and recently visited India on a British Council reading tour * SHAMS FARIDI is a prolific poet in Urdu * SHAMSUR RAHMAN FARUQI lives in New Delhi and edits the Urdu literary magazine, *Shabkhun* * BALWANT GARGI is a well-known Punjabi dramatist * SISIRKUMAR GHOSE, author of many books on literature and mysticism, is Professor of English at Viswabharati U., Santiniketan * RODNEY HALL, a leading Australian writer, has published a *Selected Poems* culled from his eleven collections * SUKHPAL VIR SINGH HASRAT, author of several volumes of poetry, lives and works in Chandigarh * A. D. HOPE is emeritus Professor of English at National U., Canberra, Australia * BIBEK JENA (b. 1935) has published one book of poetry in Oriya. He lives in Jaipur where he holds the post of Deputy Accountant General * DHRUVAKUMAR JOSHI (b. 1949), who teaches English in a Bombay college, has published two volumes of poetry * ADIL JUSSAWALLA (b. 1940) writes poetry in English and has edited an anthology of new Indian writing for Penguin Books * LAKSHMI KANNAN, a research associate at the Indian Institute of Technology, New Delhi, has published two volumes of poetry in English and several short stories in Tamil * KERSY D. KATRAK works as an advertising consultant in Bombay; he has published two collections of poetry * J. L. KAUL has translated many Kashmiri poems into English * CHANDRAKANT KHOT (b. 1940) won the Maharashtra State Award in 1969 for his poems, *Martik* * AJIT KHULLAR, Senior Lecturer in English at Dayal Singh College, U. of Delhi, is author of *A Lone Bone On Fire*, Writers Workshop, Calcutta * K. K. KHULLAR writes poetry in Urdu and works with the Ministry of Education, Government of India * ARUN KOLATKAR works as a graphic artist in Bombay; his first book, *Jejuri*, was published by Clearing House, and he has also published a collection of poems in Marathi * GORDON KORSTANGE teaches at Wesleyan U. * DAYA KRISHNA, Professor of Philosophy and former Pro-Vice-Chancellor at the U. of Rajasthan, Jaipur, is author of several philosophical works * S. KRISHNAN is a program adviser at the American Center, Madras * SATI KUMAR (b. 1938) writes in both Hindi and Punjabi and has translated Indian poetry into Bulgarian * SHIV K. KUMAR (b. 1921), who has taught at many colleges in the U.S., is currently at Franklin & Marshall College, Pa. He has published several collections of poetry, short fiction, and a novel, *The Bone's Prayer* * ALI MOHAMMED LONE has edited the Kashmiri section of *Indian Poetry Today*, published by Indian Council for Cultural Relations, New Delhi * PRABHAKAR MACHWE is a well-known poet, novelist, editor in Hindi and Marathi * JAYANTA MAHAPATRA, who won the Sahitya Akademi Award in 1982 for his book, *Relationship* (Greenfield Review Press), edits the literary journal, *Chandrabhaga,* from Cuttack, Orissa * KESHAV MALIK, editor of Sahitya Akademi journal, *Indian Literature,* has published five collections of verse * IQBAL MASUD is the pseudonym of a senior civil servant. He is also a film and theatre critic * JAMES MAUCH teaches at Foothill College, California, and has translated several Hindi poems into English * ARVIND KRISHNA MEHROTRA teaches English at the U. of Allahabad; his new book of poems is *Distance in Statute Miles* from Clearing House * JOSEPHINE MILES, the well-known American poet, teaches at the U. of California-Berkeley * PRASANNA KUMAR MISHRA lives in Puri where he teaches Oriya literature at the S.C.S. College * S. S. MISHA, author of many collections of poetry, works for the All India Radio * SOUBHAGYA KUMAR MISRA (b. 1941) has published four volumes of poetry in Oriya. He works as a Reader in English at the U. of Berhampur, Orissa * P. RAMA MOORTHY teaches English at the U. of Mysore * MEENAKSHI MUKHERJEE, editor of the literary magazine, *Vagartha,* teaches at the U. of Hyderabad, and is editor and translator of an anthology of Bengali short stories forthcoming from Oxford U. Press * PRANABKUMAR MUKHOPADHYAY (b. 1937) has been associated with the journal, *Krittibash* * SARATKUMAR MUKHOPADHYAY (b. 1931) has published several volumes of poetry * SHIRSENDU MUKHOPADHYAY (b. 1936), an eminent writer of Bengali fiction, is author of two novels, *Ghoon-Poka* and *Parapar.* He recently won an Ananda Puraskar Prize awarded by the *Ananda Bazar Patrika* group of papers * NADAAN is a Delhi-based Urdu poet * SUMATHEENDRA NADIG is an editor with a Bangalore publisher * DINA NATH NADIM (b. 1916) is a recipient of Soviet Land Nehru Award and has written poems in English, Urdu and Kashmiri * NAGARJUNA (VAIDYA NATH JHA), a social protest poet who was jailed in the Emergency in 1975, uses folk forms and idioms in his writing * RAJI NARASIMHAN has published novels in Delhi, where she lives and works * KUNWAR NARAYAN is a widely published, award-winning writer in Hindi * PANDAV NAYAK is a research associate at the South Asia Research Center, U. of Rajasthan, Jaipur * NIRALA (SURYAKANT TRIPATHI, 1896-1961), a well-known romantic Hindi poet, lived most of his life in Allahabad * JAMES NOLAN lived in India during 1978-79; his latest poetry book is *What Moves Is Not The Wind* (Wesleyan) * BIBHU PADHI teaches in Cuttack, Orissa * AYYAPPA PANIKER, Professor of English at U. of Kerala, Trivandrum, spent 1981-82 at Yale and Harvard on an ACLS grant * MRINAL PARDE is a young writer-editor in the Publications Department of Chandigarh U. * R. PARTHASARATHY is the author of *Rough Passage* (Oxford U. Press) and editor of several anthologies * GIEVE PATEL (b. 1940), a doctor by profession, is also a painter and playwright; he resides in Bombay * DEBA P. PATNAIK, now at Oberlin College, Ohio, has recently published *Geography of Holiness* and *Concelebration.* He is a well-known authority on photography * SALEEM PEERADINA, author of *First Offense,* teaches English at Sophia College for Women, Bombay * NA PICHAMURTI had a checkered career as a lawyer, temple executive, and writer of plays, poems, novels and short stories * AMRITA PRITAM, winner of the 1982 Bhartiya Jnanpith, has published several novels and collections of poetry; she resides in New Delhi * FRANCES PRITCHETT has just taken up a new appointment in the Dept. of Middle East Languages and Cultures at Columbia U. * PUDUMAIPPITHAN (C. VRIDDACHALAM, 1906-48) headed the new literary movement in Tamil during the Thirties; his works are known for their sharp criticism of society * RAFEEQUE RAAZ (b. 1952), whose poems have been extensively published, writes in both Urdu and Kashmiri * DIVIK RAMESH (b. 1946) teaches at a Delhi college and has published two collections of poems in Hindi * A. K. RAMANUJAN, who teaches at the U. of Chicago, is a well-known Indo-English poet * B. R. LAXMAN RAO (b. 1946), a teacher by profession, is author of *Gopi and Gandaleen,* a collection of poems * K. RAGHAVENDRA RAO teaches Political Science at Karnatak U., Dharwar, and has co-edited (with P. Lal) the anthology, *Modern Indo-Anglian Poetry* * MALATHI RAO teaches English at Miranda House, U. of Delhi; she has published two collections of short stories * RAMAKANTA RATH (b. 1934) is a widely published poet in Oriya who won the Sahitya Akademi Award. He lives in Delhi and is a senior member of the Indian Administrative Service * LILA RAY (b. 1910), an American by birth, lives in Calcutta, writes poetry in English and translates from Indian languages * SHREELA RAY, author

of *Night Conversations With None Other*, lives in Rochester, N.Y. *
JOHN REPP is a typesetter living in Mt. Pleasant, Michigan * The poetry
of MRIGANKA ROY (b. 1925) is marked by lyricism * PADMA SACHDEV
is a well-known Dogri poet whose first collection of poems won the 1971
Sahitya Akademi Award * VIJAY DEV NARAIN SAHI (b. 1924) teaches
English at the U. of Allahabad * GULZAR SINGH SANDHU is a Punjabi
short story writer * ASHIS SANYAL (b. 1938) has published several collections of poetry in Bengali and has translated African poetry into Bengali *
BALAKRISHNA SHARMA ("NAVIN," 1895-1961) is a well-known name
in Hindi literature. He joined the Indian National Congress in 1920, worked
actively in the Independence Movement and spent several years in prison
* I. K. SHARMA, who has translated Rajasthani poetry into English, teaches
at the U. of Rajasthan, Jaipur * R. K. SHARMA co-edits *Rajasthan Journal
of English Studies*, a bi-annual of creative and critical writing * MANOHAR
SHETTY's first book of poems, *A Guarded Space*, was published recently
by Newground, Bombay * G. S. SHIVARUDRAPPA (b. 1926) is Professor of annada Literature at Bangalore U. * SIDDALINGAIAH, a
lecturer in Kannada at Bangalore U., is himself a Harijan; the caste is still
victimized frequently by atrocities * HARIBHAJAN SINGH (b. 1919),
winner of Sahitya Akademi Award in 1969, is Professor of Punjabi at the
U. of Delhi * KEDARNATH SINGH (b. 1934), a leading Hindi poet,
teaches Hindi at the Jawaharlal Nehru U., Delhi * KHUSHWANT SINGH
(b. 1915) made his writing debut with a collection of stories called *The
Mark Of Vishnu*, followed by the well-known novel, *Train To Pakistan*; he
has also written a number of works on Sikh history, and presently edits *The
Hindustan Times* * MOHAN SINGH, a well-known romantic poet, had a
long career as poet and editor * PRITAM SINGH, poet and scholar, works
at Punjab U., Chandigarh * SAMIR PUNIT SINGH, age 12, was born in
N.Y. City, and is now a student at St. Xavier's School, Jaipur * SHAMSHER
BAHADUR SINGH (b. 1911) has written poetry in Hindi and Urdu *
JOHN TAGLIABUE's earlier poems about India appear in *The Buddha
Uproar* (Kayak Press); he teaches at Bates College in Maine * RABIN-
DRANATH TAGORE (1866-1941) won the Nobel Prize for literature
for his book of poems, *Gitanjali* * VALLIKANNAN (R. S. KRISHNASWAMY,
b. 1920) is author of four volumes of short stories, five novels and numerous
prose poems * O. J. VIJAYAN, a cartoonist by profession, lives now in
Delhi. He has written a highly original novel in Malayalam * VINDA (G.
V. KARANDIKAR) is a leading figure in contemporary Marathi literature.
His *Poems Of Vinda* was published by Nirmala Sadanand Publishers, Bombay
* SITANSHU YASHASCHANDRA (b. 1941), a well-known Gujarati poet
and critic, is at present Director of the Sahitya Akademi project on the En-
cyclopedia of Indian Literature.

Amritjit Singh & David Ray

The Editors:

AMRITJIT SINGH is Professor of English at the U. of Rajasthan, Jaipur. A widely travelled scholar, he has taught at colleges and universities in Delhi, New York City and Hyderabad. He is author of *The Novels of the Harlem Renaissance* (1976) and has co-edited *Afro-American Poetry and Drama* (1979) and *Indian Literature in English* (1981) as part of the Gale Information Guide series. He is currently at work on a bibliographic monograph on Afro-American fiction, and a collection of literary essays.

DAVID RAY, editor of *New Letters,* spent 1981-82 as an Indo-U.S. Fellow and Visiting Professor of English at the U. of Rajasthan, Jaipur. His Selected Poems, *The Touched Life,* has been published by Scarecrow Press (1982), and he has recently received the 1982 N.T. Veatch Award from the U. of Missouri for outstanding research and creative activities. He has completed a manuscript of poems about India, entitled *The Maharani's New Wall,* as well as a book of love poems translated from the ancient Prakrit.